WITHDRAWN

SINGLE MOM SYNDROME

Rising Above the Challenge with God's Help

Single Mom Syndrome
Rising Above the Challenge with God's Help

Alice Monterio

amonteriopublishing.com

or ...

SEEKING MY SAVIOR?

Copyright © 2013 by Alice Monterio

Single Mom Syndrome: Rising Above the Challenge with God's Help
by Alice Monterio

Printed in the United States of America

ISBN 9780615775692

All rights reserved solely by the author. The author guarantees all contents are original and do not infringe upon the legal rights of any other person or work. No portion of this book may be reproduced, stored in a retrieval system, or transmitted in any form or by any means—electronic, mechanical, photocopy, recording, or any other—except for brief quotations in printed reviews, without the prior written permission of the author. The views expressed in this book are not necessarily those of the publisher.

All scripture quotations, unless otherwise indicated, are taken from THE HOLY BIBLE, NEW INTERNATIONAL VERSION®, NIV®
Copyright © 1973, 1978, 1984, 2011 by Biblica, Inc.™
Used by permission. All rights reserved worldwide.

Scripture marked NKJV are taken from the New King James Version®.
Copyright © 1982 by Thomas Nelson, Inc. Used by permission. All rights reserved.

Scripture marked KJV are taken from the King James Version.
The KJV is public domain in the United States.

Cover Design and Author Photograph: Jordan Moureau
Additional Interior Layout: AJ Design and Marketing, LLC

Dedication

In memory of my brother, Harry Michael Monterio, who is gone, but never forgotten.

*The widow who is really in need and left all alone
puts her hope in God
and continues night and day to pray
and to ask God for help.*

1 Timothy 5:5

Contents

Prologue . . . . *xv*

Introduction . . . . *xvii*

Part I.   The Syndrome

          Chapter 1: Not So Wonderful News? 25

          Chapter 2: Oops ... Here He Is! 39

Part II.   Seeking My Savior

          Chapter 3: What Was I Thinking? 45

          Chapter 4: Know Who You Are 55

          Chapter 5: Sex, Relationship and Love—Oh Yea! 65

Part III.   Cosseted Under His Wing

          Chapter 6: Like a Hen that Gathers Her Chicks 85

          Chapter 7: Turning to Elisha. 95

          Chapter 8: An Amazing Gift. 107

Part IV.   Living Beyond Vision

          Chapter 9: The Powerful Seven 123

          Chapter 10: Applying the Principles 131

Prologue

Forever Family

Like a puzzle, when one member is missing, it's not complete.
Different talents and different strengths working together in harmony.
Each one is distinct from the other.
One is generously giving, seeing a need and fulfilling it,
while kindness overflows.
The other has unwavering strength that can't be torn down,
but at the same time, is gentle and humorous.
Still the other is headstrong and aggressive,
softened with understanding and compassion.
And then, amazingly, we are blessed with another
to lighten the mood with affection,
giggles and silly antidotes,
and ironically bestowed with a spirit of insight.
When we come together, we can make great things happen.
Collectively, we get the job done, like means to an end.
We've been through many storms;
some more intense than others,
but like a mighty tower grounded with a secure foundation,
we are still standing strong and tall.
We support each other and lift one another up.
Our strong point? Many things!
BUT the greatest ingredients that we possess are
love and faith in our Heavenly Father above.
The power of our love for each other, we don't even realize.
No one, or no thing, can break us or keep us down.
Why? Because, collectively, we abound.
We are a Family!

Introduction

Single Mom Syndrome was obviously written for single moms, but applies to single dads, as well. Many of us get into complicated situations, often because we don't listen to our Heavenly Father. His rules are so simple, but so difficult to follow. Why are they so difficult? There are a couple of reasons:

1) Jeremiah 17:9 reads, *"The heart is deceitful above all things. And desperately wicked: Who can know it?"*

2) James 1:14–15 states, *"But each one is tempted when he is drawn away by is own desires and enticed. Then, when desire has conceived, it gives birth to sin: and sin, when it is full-grown, brings forth death."*

Clearly, we can glean from these scriptures that the heart is deceitful, and that we are enticed by our own desires. I'm sure each and every one of us can testify to a time, or times, or many times in our lives when our weaknesses got the best of us - times when our mind said, "no", but our hearts led us astray.

We are involved in a spiritual battle, wherein the enemy attacks our weaknesses. With that said, we must wear special gear for combat. We must put on the complete suit of armor as mentioned in Ephesians, Chapter 6. One element of that suit protects the heart. It is the breastplate of righteousness (Ephesians 6:14). This breastplate—covering our hearts with righteousness—will help us make the right decisions and protect us from swaying toward what is wrong due to our weaknesses or our desperate desires. We know what is right, ponder on it, and make our decisions accordingly. As difficult as it may sound, it can be done. How do I know? Jesus would not ask us to do something that we could not do. If He says it works, it works!

Let me set the record straight, I do not condone diverting from God's original plan for family—husband, wife, and children. However, the fact remains that single parent homes do exist today and for many different reasons. You may have been married, had children, then gotten divorced; maybe you were left by a spouse. Perhaps you were married and your husband passed away, now you are the head of your household. Or, you may have had premarital relations and became pregnant, in which case, if you do God's will, you'll avoid falling into that situation. We'll examine each case more closely. God's will is for us to abstain from fornication; however, you may have already succumb to weakness, now you are carrying a child. It is not an ideal situation, but for many, this is tragic. They feel they cannot handle being a single parent for different reasons. Maybe they are too young; maybe they don't have much money; maybe they are ill; maybe they are frightened; maybe they are in college or have a career they don't want interrupted; or maybe they just don't want the responsibility. They see it as a negative, like it's a disease, hence the title Single Mom Syndrome (a.k.a. SMS). Not only has this syndrome resulted in innumerable abortions, but countless acts of crime and violence toward newborns and children, as well ... just turn on the news.

What we fail to realize is that, if we had sexual relations outside of the marriage arrangement and became pregnant, Jesus does not hate us. He does not give up on us or throw us to the wolves. He does, however, want us to repent and not continue in that course. Regardless, He absolutely loves us, and He loves our unborn child. You may be asking, "How can Jesus hate sexual immorality, but love someone born from the act?" Well, that is just the kind of God that we serve. We may not understand it, but we don't have to; we do understand that Jesus is love, and He loves children—the born and the unborn.

Let's read Matthew 19:13–15 to see how He felt about children:

> *"Then people brought little children to Jesus for him to place His hands on them and pray for them. But the disciples rebuked them. Jesus said, "Let the little children come to me, and do not hinder them, for the kingdom of heaven belongs to such as these." When he had placed His hands on them, He went on from there."*

Now what about the unborn? The undeveloped fetus is actually someone to Him. God knows that child before he or she is conceived and has a plan for them. Jeremiah 1:4–5 reads, *"Then the word of the L*ORD *came to me, saying: 'Before I formed you in the womb I knew you; Before you were born I sanctified you; I ordained you a prophet to the nations.'"*

Yes, in his mother's womb, Jeremiah was ordained a prophet!

A newly conceived child in your belly may be a fetus to you, but to God ... a warrior; a prophet; a teacher of His Word; a leader; a doctor who will heal someone; a lawyer who will cause justice to prevail; a person who will say just the right thing to turn someone's life around; or a person who may save another person's life. We don't know! We don't know the plan that God has for a "fetus". A fetus can grow into a strong man or woman and make a difference. They may be a blessing to someone as a child. They may be a blessing to you. Therefore, I believe we have no right to abort anyone ... no right. We became pregnant; now we are responsible for caring for that child, or allowing a loving family to adopt the child, but we do not have the authority to take a life. He or she is not our child, but a child of God; we are merely privileged to care for them. Will we have to care for them alone? No. Should we be afraid? No.

Let's look at another scenario. Perhaps you were married, now divorced. There are so many, many reasons why people divorce. I truly believe that married couples should do everything in their power—in God's power—to stay together. One reason that God's Word gives to divorce is, if adultery is committed. Another reason is, if an unbelieving mate leaves their spouse. In which case, the believing spouse is called to peace. Other than that, marriages should be worked on diligently to last, by both husband and wife. Both parties have to want to make it work. Reading the Bible for counsel, in addition, seeking a therapist or marriage counselor can help. Unfortunately, many people don't use these resources; therefore, the child or children involved end up living with either their mom or their dad.

I do believe that both parents must care for their child, whether together or apart. It is a sin to abandon your children.

> *Anyone who does not provide for their relatives, and especially for their own household, has denied the faith and is worse than an unbeliever.*
>
> 1 Timothy 5:8

Unfortunately, countless millions of people do not take heed to God's Word and, ultimately, suffer the consequences.

Let's examine yet another scenario. Perhaps you are married, and your spouse passes away. You have become, by unforeseen circumstances, a single parent. You have the responsibility of raising children on your own. This, I can say, is one of the most difficult scenarios. I have not personally experienced it, but I have seen others try to cope with such a loss.

In any one of these cases, there is a single parent that bares the responsibility of raising the child or children. Do they bail out on their children? No, they do not. Are they alone? No, they are not. Believe it or not, Jesus is with them.

Jesus becomes all things to all people. He loves you and your children, and He, as sure as I am sitting here writing my story, will help you. If you turn to Him, He will most certainly supply you with what you need, and beyond, to care for your children. He will not leave you or forsake you. Trust Him.

And when, or if, Jesus decides to bless you with another partner, it will be someone who is perfect for you and your child. Keep in mind, James 1:17: *"Every good gift and every perfect gift is from above, and comes down from the Father of lights, with whom there is no variation or shadow of turning."*

This book is about the syndrome of thinking that being a single parent can't be successfully accomplished…no matter how you got there, which is completely false. Also, it is about turning to Jesus for help and receiving that help. Finally, you will read about the many blessings and joy that can be obtained in single parenthood.

I hope that my experiences, trials, and triumphs change your *perception* on single parenthood and help you find peace and joy in your circumstances.

Part I

The Syndrome

Chapter I

Not So Wonderful News?

It was a day of normality, just a routine check-up at the doctor's office. I sat on the examining table and waited for my gynecologist to enter the room.

"Hi Alice," he said in a friendly voice as he walked in, "How is everything?"

"Fine."

"Any problems or concerns," he probed.

"No, I feel good. Everything is great."

As he examined me, I looked up and could almost twiddle my thumbs…just the same ole', same ole'. "He'll be done in a sec, and I'll be on my way," were my thoughts.

Then he asked, "When is the last time you had your menstrual cycle?"

I answered his question then added, "It is just a few days late. That happens sometimes. I'll start any day now."

"Are you on birth control pills?"

"No, I'm not."

Seeking clarification, he repeated, "Your cycle hasn't started yet, and you do not take birth control."

I just stared at him with a questionable, "What are you implying? He can't be serious. I know he doesn't suspect I'm pregnant. No way, impossible! I'm forty years old, okay? I am too old to conceive." Well, I guess I missed the sex education class that taught as long as you have menstrual cycles, you can conceive. Or, was I just too in denial to think I could actually get pregnant at my age? How naïve.

In any case, I blew it off and didn't think anything further about his inquisition.

"Okay, you can get dressed. I'll be right back."

He walked out to routinely do the things that doctors do when they leave you in a room for fifteen minutes, just to come back and say, "Okay, everything is fine. See you next year."

What I did not know is that he took it upon himself to perform a test that I would never expect him to perform. He did not share his plan with me.

After I had time to dress and, if I wanted to, re-dress and re-dress again, he walked back in, looked at me, paused for a moment and said, "I have good news, and I have bad news."

"First tell me the good news, then the bad."

"The good news is, you are in good health."

Okay, so I don't get it. What could the bad news be? I had NO clue. It never even entered my mind.

"The bad news is, you are pregnant; or, maybe it's good news to you."

I'm Cape Verdean, therefore, my skin has much pigmentation, but at that moment, I'm sure I turned as white as a sheet. My mouth dropped, and I was in a bit of shock.

"No, I can't have a baby. I just can't. You see, I've been a single mom … forever. My youngest is in her last year of high school. I'm supposed to be done. I cannot start all over again! I can't go through with raising a child on my own again. It is just really, really hard," I pleaded with him as though he could go back and change the test results.

"I understand."

As he displayed sympathy for me, he handed me a pamphlet and said, "If you feel like you don't want to have this baby, here's a place you can contact regarding an abortion."

I took the pamphlet, with a feeling of taboo, and said, "Thank you."

During the drive home, my mind was racing. I was talking to Jesus and just rambling on and on about how I could not do this again.

"Jesus, I cannot have this baby. I cannot do this! I know that I should not get an abortion, but Jesus; you know what I've been through. You know I don't make a lot of money, and I will have to struggle to take care of this child. And, you know I'm not the greatest mom because I don't always make the best decisions. I cannot do this! Please, please help me!"

Isn't it funny that after we go against God's will and get into 'sticky' situations, we want help from Him? And, He is so loving and so gracious that He extends Himself to us even though we messed up! Now you know that if I were following God's Word, as I ought to, this would not have ever happened. Sometimes we fall prey to our deepest desires, no matter how detrimental. Anyway, I wasn't thinking of all that at the time. All I knew is I was pregnant, and I did not want to be pregnant. I wanted it to just go away.

When I arrived home, I immediately went to my daughter's room and sat on her bed.

"Alisha, I have to tell you something."

She sat next to me and attentively listened.

I didn't beat around the bush; I just came out with it.

"I'm pregnant."

Her mouth dropped, and she burst out laughing, hysterically.

"Alisha! This is not funny! I'm pregnant!"

I could not understand how she could laugh or take it so lightly when I, on the other hand, felt like the world was coming to an end.

Comprehending my fright, she stopped laughing.

"Okay, so what do you want to do?"

"I don't know. I don't want to have this baby."

She didn't sway me one way or the other.

The next person I told was the dad. I went over to his apartment, and I said, "I just came from the doctor's. I'm pregnant."

"No, you're not; you're lying."

"I am pregnant. Honestly."

Initially, he was in complete denial. I can't say I blame him because so was I, at the onset.

I walked home, which was right across the parking lot (convenient for getting impregnated), sat on my couch, and felt very empty and alone. Shortly after, he came over and sat next to me on the couch.

"Are you really pregnant?"

"Yes, I am. I'm not going to keep it though. I'm thinking of getting an abortion."

"No, you cannot get an abortion. Please do not get an abortion. I'll be here for you. I'll help you with the baby."

He begged and pleaded with me not to get an abortion. He swore up and down that he would be there for us.

As the days proceeded, I could not see his promise being fulfilled. I did not believe him and continued with the thought of not having the baby. I prayed and I cried, and I prayed some more.

I called my sister, Kathy. Her philosophy was, "You cannot get an abortion. You have to have this baby. Don't worry. You can do it alone. The guy has nothing to do with the baby, anyway." She, too, was a single mom, so it was not a big deal to her. Not having a dad around was no reason to not have the child…minor detail.

Still struggling with it and looking for an answer from Jesus, I received a letter—saturated with guilt—in the mail. My sister, Kathy, wrote pleading with me to keep the baby, and she said that I absolutely had to and that it was against God to get an abortion. I already knew that, but she was putting it 'in my face', so to speak. I truly did appreciate her letter, but it made me more confused. However, I knew she was right.

I had other opinions, of course. When my co-workers found out, one of them said, "Alice, it is understandable if you get an abortion. You are too old to have a baby. It's going to be very difficult." I was a bit taken aback by that comment coming from my co-worker and never would have expected it. I truly did not appreciate it, even though I was contemplating it myself.

Then there was my good friend at the time (or so I thought) who had her own spin on it. I went to visit with her, and she gave me her view.

"Alice, you cannot keep this baby. You have to get an abortion. I'll go with you. You have to think about your age; what about your career?"

What career? I was a customer service representative in a call center who could not even get promoted no matter how hard I tried. I was taking college courses. I guess she was concerned with my 'possible' future career.

A common thread with these two opinionated people was my age. Well, I wasn't too old to get pregnant, so obviously, I wasn't too old to give birth.

On the other hand, another dear friend of mine, Tamatha, was totally against the idea. "You cannot have an abortion," she stressed, "It's a life inside of you."

"Tamatha, I really think I'm going to do it. I just don't want to have a baby."

"Alice, just think about it."

Well, I did think about it, and pray about it, and think about it, and pray about it.

In the back of my mind, I knew I would be accountable if I did such a thing. You see, years ago, in 1986, I got pregnant by my husband, at the time. It was our fourth child, and we had just gotten back together from being separated for six months. When he found out I was pregnant, he became furious.

He screamed at me, "You are going to get an abortion! We are not having this baby."

I looked at him in disbelief and replied, "What are you saying?"

That was just unheard of to me. I never imagined he would go there, but he was serious! I told him flat out, "No!" I meant what I said and said what I meant, but that didn't matter. He was louder than me! He was bigger than me! He was more aggressive and mean! He forced me to have an abortion. I felt that I had to go through with it. I cried ... oh, how I cried. He wanted the abortion, but I had to do everything. I had to look for the clinic, and I had to call to make the appointment.

We were told to go to the clinic the night before the procedure. When we arrived, they escorted me to one of the rooms (I guess you could call it the "killing room") and mechanically explained everything to me.

"Today, we have to insert this little disc in you, so you can dilate. By tomorrow, you will be opened enough for the procedure. Here is the table you will lay on, and this is the vacuum that we will use. It shouldn't hurt very much, but you will feel a lot of pressure. You will feel a little cramping in your belly afterward. When the procedure is complete, you will go into the recovery room for thirty minutes, and then you can go home. Make sure that someone comes with you because you will not be able to drive right after. Here are two Valiums," as she stretched out her hand to release them in mine. "Take them just before you come with something light, like toast. It will relax you. Any questions?"

Ugh, "no."

You can go use the restroom first, and then we will get started. I went into the restroom, sat on the floor and cried my eyes out.

"Jesus, please forgive me for what I am about to do. I don't want to do it, but I have to. I know it is wrong, and I am begging you to please forgive me."

The next morning arrived. I remember what I had on. It was a yellow and black sweat shirt and a pair of jeans. I sat at the breakfast table, toast in plate and two Valiums squeezed tight in the palm of my hands, so tight that it left fingernail marks in my skin. I opened my hand, looked down at the Valium, and decided I was not going to take them. I stuffed them in my pocket. After I ate my toast, we left. The entire thirty-minute ride was somber. I felt as though I was going to a funeral, and I was already in mourning. Don't let anyone tell you that when you abort a baby, you don't mourn. It is NOT true! I mourned for a very, very long time. I blackened that day in my calendar with ink and kept it for years. It was September 1986. I remember it was during a weekday because I took the day off from work and my other children were in school.

When we got there, the "nurse" led me back into the "killing room".

"Did you take your Valiums?"

"No."

"You're brave."

I took off my bottoms and lay on the table. After she set me in position, the procedure began. I had no anesthesia, no Valium, no happy gas ... nothing. I could hear the loud suction of the vacuum, and then I could feel discomfort and pressure applied to my abdomen. The entire procedure lasted for about ten minutes. I never saw my baby's disassembled body parts that were collected for disposal (I've since learned that the suction pulls apart the fetus' body).

Following the abortion, I was instructed to get dressed, handed a maxi-pad, and was led to the recovery room where I sat in a recliner and bled. My ex-husband sat beside me, expressionless.

During the ride home, again silence, but a new kind of silence ... my child was now, officially, dead. When we arrived home, I went downstairs to lie down. My husband shuffled around the room, getting his work clothes on. He then threw on his hat.

"Where are you going?"

"I'm going to work!"

"I want you to stay with me. I need you here."

"I'm not staying with you. I have to go to work!"

Don't you know that he left me there, all alone? I just had an abortion. I was ill and emotionally depressed. I had terrible cramps in my stomach.

I began to cry when he left. How could he be so cold and so cruel? Well, unbeknown to me, he was using heavy drugs at the time. I suppose the state of numb would be considered normal.

About twenty minutes later, I heard my mother holler from upstairs, "Alice, you down there?"

"Yes."

"Why did you stay home? You don't feel well?"

"I have cramps."

"Oh, okay."

We were staying in my mom's basement at the time, and she never suspected a thing. No one knew. I didn't tell a single soul. That is not the sort of thing that you go around announcing, "Hey everyone, I'm having an abortion!" So, I carried that with me for years. Only my husband and I knew. Oh, and of course, Jesus.

What made it worse is that my older sister announced her pregnancy shortly after my episode. I gave her a baby shower while enduring the emotional pain of my loss; planning the day, ordering the cake, getting the food together, and filling out baby invitations. Then, when the day arrived, I had to put on a smile and endure watching and helping her open baby presents. I was truly happy for her, but very sad for what I had done. All the while I still hid my little secret—and the agony that came with it—and kept it all to myself.

Often, I would look at her daughter, as she was growing, and I would think "my child would be that age now." They would have been born around the same time.

If I went through with aborting this baby, it would be 100% my decision, thus 100% my responsibility. My prayer to Jesus was, "I know that if I do this, it is completely on me, and I am solely accountable. My husband made me do it before, but now there is no one forcing me. It is all my responsibility; and I don't think you would forgive me that easily this time." I felt forgiven for the past, but this would be a whole new deal.

In my constant conversations with Jesus, He was presently with me, speaking to my heart to draw me to the right conclusion.

One day, I was driving down the road, pondering on my situation. I mean that is all I could think about ... I had a growing baby in my tummy and time was running out. Anyway, I was driving along and suddenly a dog ran out in front of my car. Out of panic, I immediately slammed on the breaks to save that little dog's life. Then, suddenly it occurred to me. I heard a voice in my spirit say, "You will slam on the breaks to save a dog's life, but you don't feel that same panic for your baby? Is that dog's life more important than your baby's life?" *Wow!* That hit me like a ton of bricks. I felt small and very silly. It made absolutely no sense that I would save a dog, but not a human being. How foolish!

That was a pretty clear message from God, and you would think that after that, case closed, right? Nope. One more plea, as I was heading out the door for church one Sunday morning,

"Now Jesus, I really need to hear from you on this. Please give me an answer at church. Please tell me what to do."

Like He hadn't already, but He was very obliging. As soon as I walked into church, at the beginning of the service, the pastor extended an invitation to the congregation.

"If anyone has anything on their heart this morning, anything that they would like to pray about or give to the Lord, come to the altar and pray."

That was the first and last time that was ever done, since I went to that church. The pastor always (I mean *always*) invites the congregation to the alter after the service has concluded. It was like Jesus was calling me to give this burden to Him. So, that is exactly what I did. I prayed and gave it to Him.

That entire service turned out to be about babies! The opening song was about babies. The pastor's sermon was about babies and how precious children are. He gave an example of little Jessica, who was stuck in the well. Do you remember her? He expounded on how everyone fought and struggled to get her out—firemen, policemen, civilians—because she was such a precious life. "Ugh! Does this apply to my situation? Is this clear enough for you, Alice?" I knew right then it was a definitive "No" from Jesus on the abortion issue. It was that day that the reality set in on how much Jesus loves the born and the unborn. "He truly loves this baby," I thought.

However, after that I still sunk back into doubt and fear. I told Tamatha that I was spending the night over to her house because I made an appointment for an abortion at a clinic in her hometown. She was not happy, but she said, "Okay." All through the night, she tried to talk me out of it.

The next morning, we sat at the kitchen table. She looked at me and said, "You are not going, are you?"

"No, I'm not. I can't do it."

We both looked at each other and smiled.

Deep down, I never wanted to do it, and I always knew it was completely wrong, but I was frightened of playing the single mom role again. I could have made a terrible mistake out of fear.

So, I never showed up at the clinic and now "it's on" … eight months of growing and preparing. And boy, did I grow! As I contemplated, the 'dad' was not around most of the time. I found myself sitting alone at night, so I comforted myself with ice cream sundaes and banana splits from a local ice cream shop … almost every night!

Because I was over forty, I had to have an amniocentesis done. I chose to know the sex of the baby. It was a boy! The dad and I debated over a name. He wanted "Brandon" only because a female friend of his at work suggested it … how typical. Anyway, I knew that our son would be called Colby Harrison Brown. Harrison after my brother Harry … just fancied it up a bit. Plus, it sounded like a prestigious name.

Alisha was thoughtful enough to take child birthing classes with me. My other children, two older boys, were very supportive, as well. They all were excited to meet their baby brother.

Chapter 2

Oops ... Here He Is!

IT WAS LATE at night when I began to feel contractions. They were coming every fifteen minutes. They were not severe, yet; just enough to make me stop and take notice. I got out of bed and went into the living room to sit on the couch. "Ouch, here comes another. Wait, the last one hit me ten minutes ago," I thought. There came another one ten minutes later. I sat there waiting for them to get close enough to go to the hospital. Look, I had done this three times before. Babies just don't pop out that quickly. The next contraction came in five minutes. "Oh, oh, they are getting closer," I thought. Still, I wanted to make certain it was a go, so I sat patiently while I waited for the next one. "Yup, five minutes, right on the nose." I made certain that the contractions were consistent for at least twenty minutes. I now felt the need to wake up Alisha. I went into the bedroom and informed her it was time to go. While she was getting her clothes on, I sat back on the couch and continued counting the minutes between contractions.

Not long after, Alisha was ready, and we were on our way to the hospital. Once we arrived, they immediately checked me in. Alisha came with me to my room and watched as they hooked me up, IV and all. Now it was just a matter of waiting for little man to arrive ... and waiting ... and waiting.

We arrived at the hospital between 10:00 P.M. and 11:00 P.M. on March 8. On the afternoon of March 9, we were still waiting for baby. The doctor decided that Colby would need some help coming into the world, so they prepped me for a C-section. While on the operating table, Colby's father arrived, just in time to see his son being born. He watched as the doctors did their thing, and a few minutes later, Colby was here—March 9, 2001 at 4:06 P.M. weighing a healthy eight pounds, two ounces, and twenty-one inches long.

The moment I laid eyes on him, I melted. How on earth could I have given any thought to not having this child ... how? He was so precious and so beautiful! His face was perfectly round. He had glowing olive skin, dark eyes and lots of straight dark brown hair. As I looked at him, I thought, "So you are the one that Jesus loves so deeply!"—as He loves all of His children.

While in the recovery room, Colby got hungry and had to be nursed even before I got back to my room. His dad stayed with us in recovery and spent a lot of time at the hospital visiting while we were there. He seemed happy and excited to have Colby in our lives.

When we brought Colby home, we still had separate apartments. Our intentions were to be a family; therefore, we rented a house together, so we could raise Colby and eventually get married. Our living together was not working out, though; perhaps we did not have God's blessing on such an arrangement—that is not really His will now, is it? I know I was not really comfortable with it, but I did believe that we would get married. In total opposition of that, things began to take a downward turn. I did not feel secure for a few reasons, major and not so major, so I left. Perhaps my tolerance was low because I had been through so much in my first marriage. Perhaps it was him. Perhaps it was both of us. Whatever the case, it did not work. We ended up separating after only four months. Colby was nine months old. It was December, just one week before Christmas. Colby and I moved into an apartment.

On Christmas morning, with all of our furniture still at the house we moved out of, all we had were blankets on the floor and nothing else to sit on. There was no hint of Christmas. No tree, no gifts—except for Colby's new plastic baby fork ... that's it—but we were *happy*. I felt free, and I felt safe. My older daughter and son were with us as well. Being surrounded by family and peace are so much more important than *things*.

One week later, I got all of my furniture back, and I felt whole again. I could carry on with caring for Colby as a single mom. Of course, I hoped his father and I could have worked out. A complete family is always better than a broken one, and two heads are better than one. Two incomes are better than one. Two support systems are better than one.

I made one last attempt to try and make it work again. Colby's dad moved out of state, so Colby and I went to visit him. That was a complete bust. The last attempt and the last shred of hope … gone. Yes, I am definitely a single mom, again.

I'm not talking about the kind of single mom that is raising the child, but the dad is still involved in his child's life. I'm not talking about the kind of single mom that pays the bills, but the dad sends support payments and pitches in here and there. I'm not talking about the kind of single mom where the child resides in her home, but the dad picks them up every other weekend to spend time with them, and mom gets a breather. No, no, no. I'm talking about the kind of single mom who has the child living with her and pays all the bills (shelter, food, clothing, medical expenses, school fees, recreation) herself. I'm talking about the kind of single mom who gives 100% physical and emotional support to her child.

Yes, his father completely bailed. I became the main source of everything for my child, like in so many single-parent homes, the counterpart is completely nonexistent.

Colby had a few encounters with his dad up until the age of around four. He would call his dad on the phone. Of course, I would let him. I really did want him to know his dad and have a healthy relationship with him, but it just wasn't possible. He would leave messages and never get a call back. Finally, Colby asked, "Why doesn't my dad call me?" How do you answer that question? Eventually, Colby stopped asking for him all together.

As Colby grew older, he brought more and more joy into my life. He had special qualities. There was something different about him. I began to see that we had a deep spiritual connection, and as my story unfolds, you will begin to see also.

Part II

SEEKING MY SAVIOR

Chapter 3

WHAT WAS I THINKING?

HADN'T I BEEN here before? What was all the fuss? I saw my sweet angel's face and got to know him and his quirky little personality—such as him crying every time I sprinkled baby powder on his tummy, or spitting out his baby food because he is such a finicky eater, or the way he made me light up when I came home from a hectic day of work—I can't believe I fathomed the idea of not having him at all.

Sure, when I was a single parent the first time around, there were many struggles. There are *always* struggles, but haven't I gotten through every single one? The answer is, "Yes." I'm still standing.

So, why should it be different with this child?

The very day I became a single mom to my three oldest children, Jesus stepped in and took charge.

It was a night of bewilderment. We were being evicted from the residence that I, my three young children, and my abusive husband lived in. We had to be out by the very next day. It was the second move in two years. This move, however, was the end of the line. This move would change my status and my entire life. I had no idea where we were going.

Have you ever been driving along the highway and suddenly it begins to pour? The rain is so steady and so heavy that you can't see two feet in front of you. Not even the windshield wipers can keep up with the seemingly endless buckets of water pouring on the glass. You slow down and begin to panic because you can't see the next exit, or the car in front of you, or the yellow guiding line for that matter.

That's how it was for me that night. The only thing I was certain of was that my marriage was on its last breath ... and rightfully so. My children and I were no longer going to be under the same roof with an acrimonious, out-of-control, individual: their father, my husband. I lived with twelve years of abuse from an alcohol- and drug-addicted man and now it was about to end, but I had no plan.

All I could do was get down on my knees and pray, "Dear Father, please don't let me and my children be out in the cold. Please don't let us be without a home. Please find a place for us to live. Please don't leave us."

Moments after praying that prayer, the phone rang. It was my mother, who lived across the street.

"Alice, you have to move tomorrow, don't you?" she asked.

"Yes."

"Do you know where you're going?"

"Not really," I responded.

"Well, you and the kids are coming here to stay with me," she said, "but *he* cannot come with you."

She was referring to my husband.

"Okay, Ma, he won't. I don't want him to, anyway. Thank you so much."

Right out of the gate of being a single parent, Jesus scooped us up and watched over us every day thereafter. He became my Husband and the kids' Father. For the next ten years, they had no contact whatsoever with their biological dad. He was in his own little world.

God's attention was drawn to us and prayers were answered. I learned early on that I had to depend on Him for survival. I remember when we finally left my mother's house. We moved into an apartment. That was the very first time I was alone raising my children. It was all on me. My income had to sustain the four of us. Man, was that tough! I had obtained my cosmetology license while we were living with my parents, so I looked for a job at a salon. I did find one, but the pay was not enough, and I didn't have benefits for the children.

One day, I sat at the dining room table and began to pray, "Dear God, please help me find a job to support my children."

I continued, "If you want me to be single, you have to help me take care of the kids. I need to find another job. I have to make no less than ten dollars an hour, in Jesus' name I pray, Amen."

You can't get to God without going through Jesus. When you *end* your prayer in Jesus' name, wonderful things *begin* to happen.

Right after I prayed, I looked in the newspaper. I knew that when you pray, you must *act* on your prayers, so I began reading the want ads and found an advertisement for a secretary position in an office located in a neighboring town. I hopped into my car and anxiously drove to the location listed.

When I arrived, I was informed by the nice lady at the desk that they were a temporary placement agency and the job was actually at another company.

"But you can fill out an application anyway," she said.

I filled out the application and came back home. I re-sat myself at the dining room table and continued to thumb through the want ads. I was wearing my "Don't give up" attitude.

The phone rang, "Hello, Alice, do you remember me? This is Karen. We worked together at the same company years ago."

"Oh yeah, Karen, how are you?"

"I'm fine. Listen, I have a job you can interview for; it's a customer service representative position starting at eleven dollars an hour. In three months, you can become permanent and will be at twelve dollars and fifty cents an hour. Would you like me to set up an interview for you?"

"Yes," I replied as my jaw dropped.

Jesus really wanted me to stay single—He must have had a good reason—because my prayer was answered within the next hour, and the money I asked for was right on point.

In a couple of days, I went on the interview. It went well, and although the manager who interviewed me wanted to hire me, others preferred to hire the man who had more experience in that field. I was turned down. One week went by, and I was still fancying that position. "Aww, I really wish I had gotten that job," I thought over and over again.

I received another call. It was the manager who interviewed me.

"Alice, the gentleman that we hired couldn't stand sitting at a desk all day. He prefers to be out in the field. Are you still interested in the position? We would like to offer it to you."

"Yes!" I answered with no hesitation.

I finally had a secure position that would allow me to better provide for my children. However, something most unexpected happened. Two and a half months into my job, three top executives (president of the company, human resources director, and marketing director) came from South Carolina to Massachusetts. They assembled everyone into the conference room. You can imagine what was running through everyone's mind, "This can't be good."

"We have decided to close the call center here and have everything centralized in South Carolina. That's where manufacturing is, and we feel that it's in the company's best interest to house our representatives there, as well. This allows for more efficient training and updating," explained the human resources director.

Then he continued, "This certainly is no reflection on you. You have all done a wonderful job. We're going to meet with each of you, individually, and give you your options or packages."

I sat in that chair, and I felt like the walls were closing in on me and everything I went through the past two and a half months was reversing past me. Have you ever watched a movie and when something detrimental occurs, the person appears to be standing in a tunnel and their life flashes past them? Well, that's how I felt at that moment, and my initial thought was, "Jesus, what am I going to do, now? I just got this job." Then, my survival instincts kicked in, "I'm going to have to go back out, immediately, and find another job."

"Alice, can you come in the office now?"

It seemed like a long walk into the office. I was aware of every step and every motion that I took. I entered the room and sat down only to be facing three men in suits.

"Here goes," I thought.

"Alice, we've heard lots of good things about you. You're doing an excellent job," one of them said. "We have an opening for a customer service representative in South Carolina. We would like to offer you the position."

"Huh?" was my thought, which I'm sure could be read on my face.

Another chimed in, "It's really nice in our town. We're in a prime location. You have the mountains close by, and the ocean is close by, also."

"You don't have to answer right now. You can think about it. We'll fly you to South Carolina and show you around, and then you can give us your answer," said another.

They were definitely working in concert.

"Is this really happening to me?" I thought.

When I came home that evening, the first thing I did was call my sisters. Kathy said she didn't know what I should do. It was up to me. Debbie urged me to go. She said, "You have to go. You have to try something new."

I prayed about it and decided to go. When I told my kids that we were moving to South Carolina, they didn't believe me.

"No we're not, Ma."

"Are you serious?"

"Get outta here."

They each had their own response, but each was in disbelief.

I went to visit as planned. My mind was pretty much made up even before then, I think. They took me to a real estate agent and showed me some apartments. It was pretty final, obviously.

It was difficult leaving Massachusetts, leaving *home*, but I had nothing to lose, really. I didn't have a husband or career there, only my immediate family, who would always be in my life no matter where I lived.

Finally, the day came for us to leave. On the way down, we stopped in Maryland and spent the night with my sister, Debbie. While there, I got cold feet and expressed to her that I was having second thoughts. She encouraged me to continue on and promised that she and her husband would come see me in just a couple of weeks.

The next morning, we continued on our way. After driving for eight hours, we passed a sign that beamed, "Welcome to South Carolina". Shortly after we entered the state, it began to rain. After a while, it began to pour so hard, we had to pull over on the side of the road and park beneath an underpass. The trees were eerie looking, like no other trees I had ever seen. The leaves were like vines covering the trees, which gave them all different shapes. They resembled huge monsters that were standing still; that is until you passed by, after which, they would turn their green little heads and watch you enter their world.

"These trees are creepy."

"I know," my kids agreed.

We arrived at our new apartment. It was actually a newly built complex. We were the first occupants, which was very cool.

Although we were comfortable, the culture shock of moving from Massachusetts to South Carolina was a lot to bear. The beach that was "close by" was a four-hour drive. Back in Massachusetts, I could get to three or four beaches in less than five minutes. As for the mountains, they were closer, but I'm no mountaineer.

I cried almost every day for the first year. As a result, I sought counseling. My counselor told me that I still hadn't healed from my divorce, which I was not aware of, but it made sense. I had been through so much in the past several years. In 1993, I got separated. In 1995, I was freed from a controlling organization. In 1997, I moved from the North to the South, where I knew absolutely no one. Whew. That was a lot to deal with without a breather in between.

However, Jesus had always been there for me and my children. He never left us in times of need; He fed, clothed, sheltered and comforted us. We may not have always had what we wanted, but we always had what we needed. When I became pregnant with Colby, I should have called that to mind.

I call it "Living Beyond Vision." When times are looking grim, know that God is in the midst of the storm, and He will do one of two things: 1) *deliver you* immediately, or 2) *sustain you* with His grace until He delivers you. Either way, you are completely protected by Him.

Also, believe that your situation can change in an instant. You may not be able to see the greatness in front of you, but it is there. God is working things out, behind the scenes, and it *will* materialize in your life. Essentially, *living beyond vision* is having faith.

Chapter 4

KNOW WHO YOU ARE

COLBY AND I proudly sat at our author's table. We were at a festival selling and signing the children's book we wrote together, *Pep Stephen, I Live with My Mom.*

The book is about a young boy, who lives in a single-parent home. It contains the story of Colby and me.

A married couple approached our table. Colby was sitting behind the table, and I was standing in front of it with my back turned to him. I handed the gentleman a book to look at. He glanced at the front cover—he hadn't read one word of text or even glanced at the colorful illustrations—then he asked, "Do you condone this sort of thing?"

I was a bit taken aback. I didn't know what he meant, so I responded, "Well, I'm hoping this book helps a lot of kids in single-parent homes."

"No. I mean, do you condone kids being in single-parent homes? [A well-known talk show host] always fights against this sort of thing on her show, deadbeat dads, and here you are condoning it."

Gulp! I'm sure I stopped breathing for a moment, and felt a heavy weight in the pit of my stomach. My palms began to moisten and my heart began pounding.

As I reflected on that comment, I collected my thoughts. First, I don't watch anyone's talk show. I *work* all day. Second, I don't condone, nor do I condemn, the fact that some children are being raised in single-parent homes … it just *is*.

"There are many reasons why children end up in single-parent homes. I have a friend who lost her spouse due to illness, now her daughter is in a single-parent home," I responded in my defense.

"Oh no, that's not what I mean," as he rolled his eyes and shook his head.

He was being extremely negative and confrontational, and all I wanted to do was reason with him. His wife sneaked in a jab here and there, but not as offensively as her husband.

"There are different ways to become a single parent. No matter how you get there, it is still difficult. My book is NOT about the father who doesn't support his child. This book is for *children* who are growing up with one parent. It is meant to encourage them and teach them that they can be achievers no matter their circumstances."

They continued to refute me.

The more they spoke, the more drained I became; nonetheless, I tried to explain, "I don't agree with dads not taking care of their children, but I will address those issues in my next book, which I am currently working on right now."

This debate—it seemed more like an attack—lasted for a good five minutes, which felt like an hour. Finally, they threw in the towel.

"Okay, they said, "We will be sure to follow you."

Before walking away, the wife blurted out, "This is coming from two people who don't have any children."

Wow, they were quick to jump all over me, but they have no children of their own.

When they walked away, life was sucked out of me, my enthusiasm was crushed, and I was left wondering if my efforts in writing this children's book was pointless. "Did I do the right thing? Is this a bad topic?" All these doubts were racing through my mind. I wanted to just crawl under the table behind me. I stood there, still frozen, several seconds after they left. I couldn't even turn around. All of a sudden, I heard a soft, but strong, voice behind me. "I love you, Mommy." As if to say, "We are fine and you're doing great. Just keep going."

For such a small voice, it sure packed a lot of power. My posture changed from hunched to erect. It felt as though someone infused confidence back into my spirit. I was able to hold my head up again. My nine year old (at the time) heard the entire ordeal and knew I was hurting. He knew just what to say to soothe my broken spirit.

That couple was implying that *certain* single parents were inferior and infectious to society. Don't let anyone make you feel less than what you truly are, which is wonderful. Don't allow other people's negative thoughts of you become your thoughts. Do you know how *God* sees you? Let's compare the two:

Land without water is a desert. The sky without luminaries is darkness. Two slices of bread with no meat is a wish sandwich. Families without a father are dysfunctional. Well, that's what they're called anyway.

Let's consider the meaning of the word *dysfunctional*:
1) med *(of an organ or part) not functioning normally.*
2) (esp. of a family) characterized by a breakdown of normal or beneficial relationships between members of the group.[1]

It's synonymous with counterproductive, purposeless and hopeless, to name a few.

I don't believe that a single-parent home has to be dysfunctional. Yes, it is challenging, but not debilitating. If you just know your worth, believe in yourself, and take charge of your circumstances in a positive manner, you can be productive and extremely successful. In addition, *everyone* has a purpose, and we all have hope. Hope is a free gift!

Let's talk about your worth for a moment. Do you know what pure religion is? James 1:27 describes it as such:

---

[1] "dysfunctional." Dictionary.com. *Collins English Dictionary - Complete & Unabridged 10th Edition.* HarperCollins Publishers. http://dictionary.reference.com/browse/dysfunctional (accessed: March 21, 2013).

> *Pure religion and undefiled before God and the Father is this: To visit the fatherless and widows in their affliction, and to keep himself unspotted from the world.*
>
> James 1:27 (KJV)

> Dictionary.com defines *widow* as the following:
> *1) woman who has lost her husband by death and has not remarried ...*
>
> *4) a woman often left alone because her husband devotes his free time to a hobby or sport ...*[2]

In many cases, women have become widows through the death of their husband. In many other cases, women have become widows by the latter reason, but by more extreme measures; the spouse/father doesn't return at all. Their hobby—dodging responsibility—*never* ends. They're missing in action, with no support or contact. The family has been completely abandoned. Even though in some cases it's better that way (as opposed to a dad who stays around but becomes abusive), it doesn't change the fact that you live as a widow and your children as paternal orphans.

God is protective of such ones. He knows your struggles and cares for you deeply. So much so, He instructed His followers to look after the fatherless child and widows in their affliction and called it "pure religion".

---

2   "widow." Dictionary.com. *Collins English Dictionary - Complete & Unabridged 10th Edition*. HarperCollins Publishers.
    http://dictionary.reference.com/browse/widow (accessed: March 21, 2013).

In addition to knowing that God loves you, you need to be aware of your gifts and talents. They will help you support your family and give you great enjoyment, as well.

Many have difficulty figuring out what their purpose is in life. What am I good at? What should I do? *Everyone* is good at *something*.

When I was young, I would go over to my grandmother's and comb her hair. She'd call my mother on the telephone, "Tell Alice to come over and comb my hair for me," in broken English because she spoke Creole fluently—she and my grandfather emigrated from the Cape Verde Islands to the United States. My mother would tell me, and I would quickly run across the street to her house. She had long, fine, salt and pepper (mostly salt) hair.

She would send me to the kitchen, "Pour a cup of coffee and bring it to me."

There was to be no sugar or cream added, just black coffee. Back then, they used percolating pots. You know, with the clear knob on top, so you could see when the coffee turned good and black. The first time she sent me to do so, I thought she actually wanted to drink the coffee. I made sure I grabbed a nice clean cup and carefully poured from the pot. It was still lukewarm from the morning.

"Here you go, Grandma," I proudly handed her the cup.

She took it from my hand, dunked her comb in it, and told me to stroke her hair with the coffee-dipped comb. I was stunned, and I didn't quite understand why, but I followed her instructions—comb, dunk, comb—until her white strands turned brown. "That's perfect," she'd say. That was her way of dying her hair. After I combed the gray out, I would make a single braid on the back of her head then twist it in a bun and pin it up. I was so proud of my finished work! I'd get the mirror and let her see how beautiful she looked. She'd smile. That was such a special time, and it proved to be extremely satisfying to me.

I realized that I loved making her feel good about herself, and I loved working with hair, in general. It touched something deep in my spirit. Yes, it awakened my gift, a gift with which I was created. Now, I dye hair using color and developer.

When I got settled into the workforce, I went into an office setting. There, I discovered that I love typing, writing and the English language. It delights me to dig into a thesaurus for new and fascinating words.

My manager, who was hard of hearing, actually wrote a book, *Deaf Heritage*. We had the task of transcribing his taped and handwritten manuscripts into typed format. With each word, paragraph, phrase, description, and dialogue—although then, I didn't know it was dialogue—my love for writing was beginning to take root. However, it was passive because although I loved *his* book, I never in one million years thought that I could write one. Anyway, what would I ever have to write about? I had no idea that, years later, God would provide me with plenty to say.

When he published it, he made certain our names were actually printed on the inside fold of the book cover under "Acknowledgments." That was special for me. That would be the first time I see my name in print on a book cover. See how life has a way of "messing" with us?

Surprisingly enough, not only did my grandmother have me coffee-dye her tresses, she often dictated letters for me to write to her friends. Those moments resonated with me. My two passions—writing and styling hair—were in me when I was just a little girl.

I was able to supplement my income by utilizing my cosmetology skills; now I'm writing books.

If I had allowed that couple to discourage me, I wouldn't have believed in *Pep Stephen*. Because I continued to believe in the book, I sent a copy to Les Brown with a cover letter, dated November 9, 2012, explaining my intentions. On November 15, 2012, I was driving home from work and thinking, "I sure would love to speak with Les Brown. That would be so encouraging."

After my son and I arrived home, we ate dinner. Around 7:25 P.M., I intuitively walked over to my cell phone. I noticed that I received a missed call just a moment ago. I didn't hear the phone ring because it was still on silent from my workday. The number wasn't recognizable, and I never return calls to numbers that aren't familiar. However, something in me made me dial back immediately.

"Hello, you called my phone?"

"Yes, this is so and so," he made up a fictitious name. "Nah, I'm just kidding; this is Les Brown."

"No way!" I was disoriented and immediately wondered who I told about the book I sent to Mr. Brown. I thought someone was playing a joke on me, like one of my boys, but I didn't tell my boys.

My heart was racing, and I continued shouting, "No way, Les Brown is NOT calling my phone!"

I'm sure he was amused by my excitement.

"I'm calling because I'm holding your book in my hand," then he read the title with such meaning, "*Pep...Stephen...I Live with My Mom.* I lllllike this book!"

I had a grin from ear to ear. We spoke for about five minutes or so, then he had to hang up because he was about to teach a speaking class.

Les Brown is one of the top motivational speakers in the world. It was quite an honor to receive a phone call from him. The fact that he liked our children's book boosted my confidence and was affirmation that our *Pep Stephen* series serves a great purpose.

In overcoming struggles of being a single mom, I've developed empathy for other single moms. I use my God-given skills to feed my passion. I call that finding and fulfilling your purpose in life. We all have one, and everyone's purpose is to help others in some manner by using their gifts and talents. It's very rewarding.

As my sister Debbie says, "Don't let anyone plant seeds of doubt in your garden (mind) because you'll have to uproot them; no one has time for that!"

You are loved more than you know and worth more than you could imagine. Do the *best* you can; God will do the rest. He'll make the 'dys' in *dysfunctional* disappear.

Chapter 5

SEX, RELATIONSHIP AND LOVE—OH YEA!

YES I HAD to go there. That is how many of us became single moms in the first place. I call the combination of sex, relationship, and love **Sur-ReaL**. If you don't have all three, it's a nightmare and you are living a lie, as my son put it.

When he was younger, I was sitting on my closet floor sorting out some clothes. He strolled in, sat next to me, and began murmuring while playing with a little trinket he was holding. Then, out of nowhere, with clarity, "You're living a lie," flowed out of his mouth.

I swiftly looked up at him and asked, "What did you say?"

He responded, "Nothing."

He did that so many times, as you will learn in upcoming chapters. He says things. I mean, they just roll off of his tongue, and it's like the Holy Spirit is speaking to me *through* him. He never knows what he says or why he says it. It's always a profound message to me.

I knew right then it was pertaining to my relationship with a man I had been dating for a few years. Oh yea! I knew it was a lie in my heart, but I wanted a companion, so I pretended it was true. Sadly, it didn't have the *Sur-ReaL* factor, the three ingredients that make a lasting partnership. Those factors are the key formula that makes you feel like this connection is so fantastic that it must be a dream, that it's something that just doesn't happen every day. It's special and completely satisfying.

I'm not referring to a whirlwind romance, where some guy comes along and sweeps you off of your feet. Everything happens so rapidly; you feel as though you've met your soul mate and within a very short period of time, he's managed to get you to move in, get engaged or get married. You find yourself saying, "This is too good to be true. He's perfect." Yes, 99.9% of the time, it *is* too good to be true; no one is perfect. Usually, in three to six months, your partner will reveal their true colors, so hold off on the whirlwind romance.

It's like a roller coaster ride; you're whisked away and caught up in excitement. Before you know it, the ride is over; so, you step out of the once secured cart and onto solid ground, but your legs feel a little wobbly and your head is still spinning. It's all you can do to keep from upchucking the deliciously sweet cotton candy, candy apple and Italian ice you ate earlier. A fun-filled artificial relationship is similar, but worse. When it ends, you're finally planted on solid ground; however, your head is still spinning with confusion because you can't grasp what just transpired and you're left in ruins, emotionally, spiritually, and sometimes financially.

Go slow and take time to get to know the individual. In a relationship, love grows over time, then that love forms into a strong bond between two people, which eventually leads to marriage ... *and then sex*. It doesn't happen overnight—and it shouldn't.

Many couples have lots of sex, minimal relationship, and absolutely no love. That is a formula for disaster and devastation. It's painful, destructive, and a destroyer of self-esteem. You can't give your absolute best to your children if you are functioning on self-loathing. Yes, you don't love yourself very much if you are with someone who doesn't love you. In that case, you can't give 100%. You can still be a great mom; I'm not saying that you can't. What I am saying is you can't reach your full potential, if you are not whole.

Let's look at the three ingredients individually.

SEX

Sex feels good and is satisfying for oh, say about, five minutes. When there is no relationship, it feels as though you're being used and then tossed. When there is no love, you're left with an empty feeling deep inside. You can compare it to a vacuum sucking up all of your energy and all of your emotions leaving you numb. As soon as it's over, you feel nothing; no warmth, no compassion, and no love from your partner. Even still, the adrenaline high that you experience from the release of endorphins in your brain (during the act) keeps you going back for more and more, like a drug. It's a viscous cycle. You become codependent on the other person to make you feel good, even if it's for a short period of time, even if it's a lie.

What are we really giving up when we have sexual relations outside of the marriage arrangement? Freedom. You may think that you possess freedom of expression, or the freedom to do as you please, when you can "freely" have sex with someone, but what you are actually doing is hurling yourself into bondage. There is no freedom in that, whatsoever. You no longer have control over yourself, emotionally or physically.

If you are at the point where you feel like you can't concentrate without that person; or, if you feel like you would want to die if they were not in your life, it's not love; it is codependency. When someone has control over your thoughts and emotions in such an adverse manner, I repeat, *you're in bondage.*

Have you ever heard of soul ties? Unhealthy soul ties are formed when you have sexual relationships with people who don't have God's spirit. The soul is made up of mind (thoughts) and emotions (feelings).

God instituted marriage in the Garden of Eden between Adam, and Eve and within that arrangement they were to multiply and fill the earth. He designed sex to be performed within the marriage arrangement. You are giving your whole self to the other person and becoming one with them.

> *The man said, "This is now bone of my bones and flesh of my flesh; she shall be called 'woman,' for she was taken out of man." That is why a man leaves his father and mother and is united to his wife, and they become one flesh.*
>
> Genesis 2:23–24

God does not want us to have sex outside of the marriage arrangement and tells us how He feels about it in His Word.

> *"I have the right to do anything," you say—but not everything is beneficial. "I have the right to do anything"—but I will not be mastered by anything. You say, "Food for the stomach and the stomach for food, and God will destroy them both." The body, however, is not meant for sexual immorality but for the Lord, and the Lord for the body. By his power God raised the Lord from the dead, and he will raise us also. Do you not know that your bodies are members of Christ himself? Shall I then take the members of Christ and unite them with a prostitute? Never! Do you not know that he who unites himself with a prostitute is one with her in body? For it is said, "The two will become one flesh." But whoever is united with the Lord is one with him in spirit. Flee from sexual immorality. All other sins a person commits are outside the body, but whoever sins sexually, sins against their own body. Do you not know that your bodies are temples of the Holy Spirit, who is in you, whom you have received from God? You are not your own; you were bought at a price. Therefore honor God with your bodies.*
>
> 1 Corinthians 6:12–20

> *Now for the matters you wrote about: "It is good for a man not to have sexual relations with a woman." But since sexual immorality is occurring, each man should have sexual relations with his own wife, and each woman with her own husband ... Now to the unmarried and the widows I say: It is good for them to stay unmarried, as I do. But if they*

> *cannot control themselves, they should marry, for it is better to marry than to burn with passion.*
>
> 1 Corinthians 7:1–2, 8–9

It really can't get any clearer than this.

One evening, I was using one of my girlish facial products. I happened to look at the writing on the jar, which I had superficially scanned before, but this time it left an impression. It said, "Obey Your Body". Fabulous product, by the way, but that phrase got me thinking, "That's what the world would have us do, isn't it?" We don't want to obey our body because the body is filled with fleshly desires. Like the Apostle Paul, we want our body to be a slave to us, not us to it.

> *Therefore I do not run like someone running aimlessly: I do not fight like a boxer beating the air. No, I strike a blow to my body and make it my slave so that after I have preached to others, I myself will not be disqualified for the prize.*
>
> 1 Corinthians 9:26–27

We want to have control of our members. In doing so, we can lead a more healthy and productive life.

The benefits of abstaining from sex outside of marriage are countless. These benefits include the following: self-esteem, self-respect, confidence, *freedom* from the possibility of sexually transmitted diseases, *freedom* from unwanted pregnancy, *freedom* from being used and tossed, *freedom* from heartache and turmoil, *freedom* to meet and be with a person who *truly* loves you, *freedom* to live whole and reach your full potential, and a clear conscience before God. You may be able to think of even more. Did you notice, freedom … freedom … freedom … freedom … freedom … freedom? Yes, freedom, as opposed to bondage.

Relationship

The root word of relationship is *relation*. Merriam-Webster.com defines *relation* in the following ways:

> *2 : an aspect or quality (as resemblance) that connects two or more things or parts as being or belonging or working together or as being of the same kind …*
>
> *7 a : the state of being mutually or reciprocally interested (as in social or commercial matters) …*[1]

Notice the operatives here: *working together; being of the same kind; being mutually or reciprocally interested.* Clearly, a relationship is a two-way street. It involves togetherness (on the same page), and it is reciprocated (returned).

If *you* find yourself in a relationship, but *your partner's* participation is slack, it's not a good sign. If you find yourself more concerned for his welfare, than he for yours, the feeling is not mutual. If he puts you down all the time and makes you feel like you are not good enough, he is not interested in your well-being. If he doesn't support what you do and your future goals, this is detrimental to your growth. All these behavior patterns do not spell r-e-l-a-t-i-o-n-s-h-i-p. He is not reciprocating your feelings and support toward him.

When you are in a real relationship you do things for each other,

---

[1] "relation." *Merriam-Webster.com.* 2013.
http://www.merriam-webster.com/dictionary/relation (March 22, 2013).

respect one another's opinions and values, listen to one another, and try to please the other person. You encourage one another. You have things in common. You are like-mannered and like-spirited. You fit together like two pieces of a puzzle. It just works.

A dear friend of mine, and single mom, Tara, who is happily engaged to be married, described a true relationship like this:

> *If you have to ask yourself, "Am I in a good relationship," then you are probably not in a good one. When you are treated the way you would treat any loved one, you know you are with someone that is worth your time. Once you find someone that actually puts you before themselves ... that considers your feelings first ... that genuinely wants to learn everything about you ... what makes you, you ... and then actually shows you how much they appreciate you, you will then know you found a good guy. And, the effort to make you happy will never fade. The effort he puts towards making the relationship work will be just as great as your effort. It's a partnership.*

So, there you have it!

LOVE

Love is the thing that ties it all together. It's the glue that binds you. Love is simple. The Apostle Paul describes it like this:

> *Love is patient, love is kind. It does not envy, it does not boast, it is not proud. It does not dishonor others, it is not self-seeking, it is not easily angered, it keeps no record of wrongs. Love does not delight in evil but rejoices with the*

truth. It always protects, always trusts, always hopes, always perseveres. Love never fails.

1 Corinthians 13:4–8

What more can you say about love?

A man who truly loves you will develop a deep and meaningful relationship with you. He will *actually* marry you and wait to make love to you after you become his wife.

If you don't have all these elements with your partner, especially love, which makes everything else fall into place causing you to have a *Sur-ReaL* sensation, walk away.

Many men, who pursue women for the sport of it, know what they are doing. They know that when you give into their shenanigans, you are sabotaging yourself.

Consider some definitions of the word *sabotage*:

3 a: an act or process tending to hamper or hurt

b: deliberate subversion[2]

Let's also look at the word *subvert* (the verb form of *subversion*):

1 : to overturn or overthrow from the foundation : ruin

2 : to pervert or corrupt by an undermining of morals, allegiance, or faith[3]

---

2   "sabotage." *Merriam-Webster.com*. 2013. http://www.merriam-webster.com/dictionary/sabotage (March 22, 2013).

3   "subvert." *Merriam-Webster.com*. 2013. http://www.merriam-webster.com/dictionary/subvert (March 22, 2013).

I was conversing with one gentleman I dated. I was informing him that my past relationships never turned out well. In response, he turned to me and coldly said, "Did you ever stop to think that it may be you?" Years later, I dated another gentleman who smirked at me and said, out of the blue, "You do the same thing over and over again." My heart dropped, and I discerned he was referring to the way I handle relationships. He virtually said the same thing as my former boyfriend, *years later*. They know that when you give your body to them, you are setting yourself up for failure, but they are not going to tell you your mistake because, well, then they wouldn't be able to get away with manipulation. I'm not speaking for all men. I know there are wonderful men out there, but at the same time, there are men in the world who purposely enjoy misleading women.

The Bible describes such ones in 2 Timothy, Chapter 3. I'm paraphrasing, but there it explains how the world will be in the last days (our time): People would be lovers of themselves, lovers of money, boastful, proud, abusive, unholy, without love, without self-control, brutal, lovers of pleasure rather than lovers of God, to name some. The Bible goes on to warn, *"have nothing to do with them"*. Then in verse 6, it pinpoints them more specifically: *"They are the kind who worm their way into homes and gain control over weak willed women, who are loaded down with sins and are swayed by all kinds of evil desires, always learning but never able to acknowledge the truth."*

This sounds like traits of a predator. A predator studies his prey— some can size you up in minutes—and figures out your weaknesses and your needs. Then, he'll know exactly how to approach you and what kind of persona or mask to put on for you. Were you molested or abused as a child? Do you have low self-esteem? Are you a single mom with a deep desire for a completed family? Are you extremely empathic? He can size you up by the way you walk, talk and other signals that you give off. After he has figured out his prey, he pounces. This is where he puts on the false charm and pretends to fill all those needs that you have. I say "pretends" because, he is *not* sincere. He is just setting you up for the kill. They say and do things that they know will hook you. Yes, tailored *just* for you.

Listen, just because someone spouts off terms of endearment such as, Baby, Sweetie, Honey, and Love, don't think they are any more sincere than someone shouting profanities to you.

Once they have you right where they want you, you will notice that things begin to change. "Why isn't he as sweet as he used to be? Why doesn't he treat me the same? He doesn't do *this* anymore, and he doesn't do *that* anymore. Why isn't he the same person?" Because he NEVER was that person; he only pretended to be. You see the real deal now. He doesn't pay you any attention. He lies to you, cheats on you, and degrades you with insults and name-calling. You find that your money is slipping away but can't figure out exactly how.

Predators want sex, money, power or anything else their prey may provide. Once, you've stopped supplying them with what they want, you are useless to them. If someone tells you, "People are tools," you may as well just ask, "Well, what kind of tool am I?" They have no more feelings for you, or anyone else, than they do for a hammer. You are merely used for their amusement or benefit. They will take you off of their tool belt, which is secured around their waist (close by for future use), do as they will with you, put you back on the belt, then pick up another handy dandy tool, and rotate back and forth. Your job is to get off of the tool belt and stay off by disconnecting yourself from the destructive person all together.

What are the traits of a predator? Here is a list (and many of these traits also indicate psychopathic tendencies): superficially charming, glib, shallow emotions, anger issues, sexually promiscuous, constant lying and deceiving (even when they don't have to), delusions of grandeur, lacks empathy, and lacks a conscience; therefore, lacks guilt. They are extremely controlling and very manipulative. They are subtle destroyers.

While they are exerting energy to control everything and everyone, ironically, they lack internal control.

They are also good at turning things around on you. When you confront them, they flip and make it seem like you are the one with the problem. You are the crazy one. They will say to you, "You're crazy!" That is their response for most any complaint that you have. Everything that *they* do wrong is twisted around and becomes *your* fault. They will make you doubt your reality. This is called *gaslighting*.

You slowly find yourself on a downward spiral and are left wondering what happened. When dealing with a person such as this, you may experience or may feel:

Angry	Lonely
Ashamed	Loss of Appetite
Confused	Loss of Sleep
Deceived	Manipulated
Depressed	Morally Compromised

Disrespected	Stressed
Empty	Trapped
Frightened	Unattractive
Frustrated	Unloved
Hurt	Unwanted
Ignored	Used

Don't bother telling them that their treatment toward you is making you feel any of these negative emotions because it will give them great joy to know that they have succeeded at making you absolutely miserable.

When dealing with such ones, you are dealing with darkness. They cannot feel what you feel. They cannot hear your cry. Their spirit cannot connect with your spirit. God said what does light have to do with darkness and darkness to do with light.

To fight against their machinations, you cannot fight with the flesh and be victorious. You are dealing with the spirit; therefore, must fight with the spirit.

> *For we do not wrestle against flesh and blood, but against principalities, against powers, against the rulers of the darkness of this age, against spiritual hosts wickedness in the heavenly places. Therefore take up the whole armor of God, that you may be able to withstand in the evil day, and having done all, to stand.*
>
> Ephesians 6:12–13 (NKJV)

You don't have to be misled; you can see them for who they really are and steer clear.

> *But they will not get very far because, as in the case of these men, their folly will be clear to everyone.*
>
> 2 Timothy 3:9

No wonder God instituted sex within the marriage arrangement. He also warned to only marry in the Lord, meaning only marry someone who loves the Lord, as you do—a child of His. When we have sex with someone outside of the marriage arrangement and someone who does not love the Lord, this soul tie that you've created can be extremely harmful to your well-being. If you find yourself in this situation, pray for deliverance. It may not come, immediately, but it will come. When it does, forgive the person who hurt you. You MUST forgive, so that you can move forward. Forgive, but don't forget, so that you don't return to a bad situation.

When it's over, and it *will* be, don't be disheartened by the silent still atmosphere that replaces the "chaotic" excitement that was short-lived. It's similar to a tornado that unexpectedly rushes in, destroys everything in its path and then disappears, never to be seen again. Embrace it. It's your peace being restored. We serve a God of restoration. He always gives back what the enemy has stolen from us, *multiplied*.

The guy who told me I kept doing the same thing over and over again was right. I've had the same type of relationship my entire life, repeating the same mistake. I was gullible and enticed by my own desires. I wanted someone to love me, so I believed every word I was told, never coming to terms with the fact that God loves me.

I've finally figured out what I've been doing wrong. Now, I want to do it the right way, God's way. We can't keep doing the same thing and expect different results. If I applied all the Scriptures that are sited, I would have saved myself a lot of trouble and wasted time. Instead, I learned the hard way. Don't learn the hard way.

Jesus showed me that I was grieving the Holy Spirit. I'm blessed in so many ways and that always baffled me. I have a lovely home, beautiful children and a good job. God always answers my prayers, but in the area of finding someone to share my life with, it didn't happen. I prayed and I prayed, but every man that I dated proved to be Mr. Wrong. Then I started to take a closer look at myself. "Why am I blessed there, but not here?" As a result, I realized that in other areas of my life, I was actually working in harmony with my prayers, but in my love life, I was not. I'd pray, then when someone came along, Holy Spirit would show me that he is NOT the one ... no, no, no. All the signals were there and the red flags waving high and vigorously, but I would not pay attention to them and continue to date anyway. In those cases, I was grieving the Holy Spirit.

To grieve is to cause to suffer. Yes, when we don't listen to God's Word, or listen to the Holy Spirit when He is trying to direct us, we are causing the Holy Spirit to hurt. He wants so very much to help us, but He can't, if we are going against His lead. He cannot work with our resistance. That is the reason I could not be blessed in this area and, that is why I suffered unnecessarily at the hands of those who did not really care for me.

God's Word speaks concerning the Holy Spirit in these verses:

> *Yet they rebelled and grieved his Holy Spirit. So he turned and became their enemy and he himself fought against them.*
>
> Isaiah 63:10

> *And do not grieve the Holy Spirit of God, with whom you were sealed for the day of redemption.*
>
> Ephesians 4:30

I've learned not to dread being alone so badly that I'll settle for someone who is detrimental to my well-being. It's a hard lesson, so I'm writing to you, so you don't have to experience what I've been through.

If you are longing for a partner, pray for the man that God would have you marry. Be specific in your prayer, but follow the lead of God's Holy Spirit. Make certain you have all the elements of a *Sur-ReaL* relationship. Pay attention to any red flags that may be waving. This is especially essential, if you are a single mom because when you are hurting from a bad relationship your children are hurting, too.

All too often, I've seen men move in with single moms and their children or vice versa without the benefits of marriage. That is very distressing to watch because it doesn't send a moral message to your children, and it usually ends up in disaster.

When I was in a one-sided relationship, my son told me that I was living a lie. How profound, since Jesus said this:

> *But the hour is coming, and now is, when the true worshippers will worship the Father in spirit and truth; for the Father is seeking such to worship Him. God is spirit, and those who worship Him must worship in spirit and truth."*

John 4:23–24 (NKJV)

I believe that worshipping God in truth encompasses every aspect of our lives.

If a man truly loves you and your children, he will create a stable two-parent home—the right way—and be a provider for you and your children. He'll become a wonderful husband to you and a devoted father to your children. Now, isn't that what single moms really desire?

Part III

Cosseted Under His Wing

Chapter 6

LIKE A HEN THAT GATHERS HER CHICKS

Jerusalem, Jerusalem,
you who kill the prophets and stone those sent to you,
how often I have longed to gather your children together,
as a hen gathers her chicks under her wings,
and you were not willing.

Matthew 23:37

TWO YEARS AFTER I had Colby, I still struggled with depression. There was a heavy cloud that hovered over me. I couldn't get rid of it. Whenever something adverse occurred, whether great or small, I would react in the same manner—my life is falling apart … it's the end of the world … I'm doomed. It was quite a heavy burden with which to live.

One evening, I was watching an evangelist on television who was ministering healing to people in the audience.

He turned to address the television viewers, "I know there are people out there who'd like to be healed. Pray with me right now, so you can experience a miracle."

I thought, "Is that for real? Can you miraculously be healed?" I knew that Jesus healed when He was on the earth. I had no doubt about that, but was He still doing so?

I then said, "If I were going to be healed, I would want to be healed of depression."

Nothing phenomenal occurred—no sensation in my body, no falling to the floor—to indicate I was actually healed. One week later, my daughter and I were riding in the car, and I was in a really good mood. Then it dawned on me, "Alisha, I haven't gotten depressed all week."

She cocked her head to the side, then said, "That's right, you haven't."

"I was healed, Alisha!"

"What?"

"I was healed! I was watching an evangelist on T.V. who was preaching on healing, and I said that I would want to be healed of depression. I confessed it, and it happened!"

We were both amazed. I can honestly say that I've never felt that dark cloud again. Sure, there are moments when I'm not super happy, or I'm upset when something goes wrong, but it doesn't last for very long. I'm able to bounce back quickly, like a normal person.

After I was healed, something even more amazing happened. One evening Colby was lying next to me, when he started whimpering, "My ear hurts." I thought, "What's to keep me from praying for him right now and he be healed? Jesus healed when He was on the earth, and I know He is still healing because *I* was healed."

So, I prayed for Colby's healing. I placed my hand on his ear and earnestly pleaded, "Dear God, please heal Colby's ear. From his head to his toe, please remove any infirmities in his body, in Jesus' name I pray, Amen." As I was praying, I felt a *pop* in my left ear, the same side that was hurting Colby. I was stunned. Colby rolled over and lay peacefully.

"Colby, does your ear still hurt?" I asked.

"No, mommy," he responded and fell fast asleep.

A week or two after that, my granddaughter wasn't feeling well. Her mom came to me and asked if I would pray for her.

Now, Alisha knew that I had been healed, and then Colby had been healed; so she had faith that her daughter could be healed as well.

"Ma, please pray for Arian," she pleaded.

"But Alisha, was it really my prayer that healed him? It really worked?"

"Yes, Ma, it did!"

Funny, even when you witness a miracle, it's hard to fathom that it really occurred in that manner. Especially, when it's from your own prayer; "God *really* answered *my* prayer … little ole' me."

I prayed the same way I prayed for Colby, and in the midst of praying, Arian displayed a sense of peace and rested her head on her mother. Minutes later, she was playfully jumping up and down on the bed.

A couple of months later, I called my sister. It was the day before Thanksgiving. I remember because she was concerned about eating with her family the next day. Debbie suffered from a problem with her TMJ (lockjaw). Periodically, it would sneak up on her; it would continue to hurt and progress to the point where she couldn't move her jaw. The pain would last for a couple of weeks before subsiding.

When I called, she happened to be in a grocery store.

"Alice, I'm so glad you called. My jaw is starting to hurt me, and I won't be able to enjoy Thanksgiving tomorrow. Please pray for me. "

"Okay, Debbie, we'll pray right now."

I prayed just as I did previously. Her discomfort didn't disappear immediately, but she expressed confidence in her healing.

That night, before I went to bed, I was compelled to pray again. I got down on my knees and pleaded with God to heal my sister. Tears were rolling down my cheeks, I wanted it so badly.

The next day, I called my sister to check on her condition.

"Alice, I feel great. I'm talking and laughing and eating. The pain is completely gone."

"Deb, does this usually happen? Does it usually just go away?"

"Never! Once it starts, it keeps getting worse until it runs its course."

She was healed and has never experienced TMJ problems again.

Jesus is super good. He does nest you under his wing, and He is there in every situation. When you are sick, He heals or comforts. When you're in financial straits, He provides. When you're car breaks down in the middle of the highway—and that has happened to me a couple of times—He scoops you up.

Recently, Colby and I were driving home from my oldest son's house. It was an hour drive, and it was late at night. The roads were desolate. Five minutes from my house, we stopped at a red light. When the light turned green, I stepped on the gas pedal to proceed. That's what you do at a green light, you go. Well, we didn't go. The car wouldn't move. I stepped on the gas again. The motor was running, but the car wouldn't accelerate.

My body wanted to go limp, but my mind kept recalling all the times God stepped in and rescued me from situations. Colby began to whimper.

"Don't worry. We're okay, Colby."

We weren't sitting there for two minutes when a van pulled up beside us. They rolled down their window. The gentleman leaned over from the driver's seat and asked, "Do you need help?"

"Yes, we do. My car won't move. Can you please help me push it off the road into that parking lot?"

"Sure."

He got out of his car to help me. His wife took the wheel and drove their car into the parking lot, as well. He pushed with all his might, and I'm certain Angels were helping.

Once my car was secured in a parking slot, I wasn't ashamed to ask, "Can you please drop us off at home. I literally live five minutes from here."

He had to think a moment, "Well, okay. I have to make room in the car. My mother, wife and two kids are in there, but I'm sure you and your son can squeeze in the back seat."

We fit like a glove. We talked during the drive, and I was home so quickly that they sat, for a moment, in front of my house while we finished our conversation.

"I'm a pastor," he said.

"Really?"

I was amazed that it was a pastor who 'happened' to stop and help us late at night.

"I'm a Christian and an author. I wrote *Saved by Grace, A Gift from God*, which was published in 2007," I told him a little about myself.

His eyebrow raised and his wife said, "Ahh."

"I would really love to get a copy of your book," he said.

Then, he hesitated for a moment, "You know, my father is a mechanic. I can bring him to your car tomorrow and have him take a look at it."

"I don't want to inconvenience you."

"It's no problem at all. Call me in the morning, and we'll figure out a time."

I was elated. I knew God had put this wonderful family in our path.

The next morning arrived. I called him and left a message. He called me back shortly after.

"Hello."

"Hi Alice, how are you today?"

"I'm good, thanks."

"My father and I will be over in about fifteen minutes. We can just pick up the key from you and go to the car, if you're busy and don't want to go out."

"I'm not really busy, but yea, that will be fine."

He picked up the key and went to my car. When they returned, they informed me that they could not get my car to move, and that it would have to be towed. I expected as much.

"Thank you so much. Write down your address. I'll send you a copy of my book."

He was very cordial and wished me the best with my car situation.

The next day, I called an auto repair company. Since they had the car in their possession, they performed a diagnostic test. Waiting to hear the results was unnerving. One year prior, I spent one thousand dollars replacing a converter. I was hoping it was not going to cost that much, but at the same time, I was prepared for that news.

The phone rang, "Alice, there is something broken in the transmission. It will cost over three thousand dollars to repair."

My heart sank to my feet and my jaw dropped. God has a plan; I just know He does. I *had* to believe.

"Uh, okay."

"Sorry to have to give you bad news," he said.

"Well, I don't think I'm going to repair it at this point. With almost two hundred thousand miles on the car, I'm going to keep sinking money into it. My son and I need something that's not going to break down on us. I think I'm just going to replace it."

"Okay, let us know what you want to do."

I went online and perused cars that I like from one particular dealer. I gave them a call. A pleasant man with an accent answered the phone.

"Hi, I'm looking into purchasing a car."

"Well, what kind of car do you want?"

I gave him the make and the model of the car that I had seen on their website.

"Give me some of your information now, and I'll call a finance company to see if we can get you approved."

I gave him the information, and we hung up. Ten minutes later, he called me back. I didn't expect to get an answer so quickly.

"You were approved for that car."

He informed me of the down payment that was required, which was very minimal ... another surprise.

Shortly afterward, I started looking up auto salvage companies, so I could sell my deceased car. I called one company, and they gave me a really low price, which is not even worth repeating. It was ridiculous.

I kept browsing the Internet, and then I came across another. "Oh, this one is owned by Tony, that's my dad's name. I'll go with that one." I have such a sentimental spot for my dad. He passed away in 2004, but I think of him every day.

When I called Tony, he was very friendly and extremely accommodating.

He asked, "How much do you want for the car?"

"I have no idea. I've never done this before."

"On a scale of one to ten, how would you rate your tires?"

"Uh, seven or eight."

He informed me that if the tires were in good condition, he would pay up to a certain amount. Yes, you guessed it! The amount he quoted was the *exact* amount I needed for my down payment.

When I arrived at Tony's establishment to make the transaction, he informed me that he didn't realize how far he had to drive to pick up my car and that he usually doesn't travel that distance. We followed him up a few stairs that led to his small office. It was personalized with pictures and wall hangings, including a New York Yankees banner. That's when I realized we had northern roots in common. From the banner, my eyes wandered the wall and fell upon a picture frame, wherein was a beautifully printed scripture:

> *The Lord is my Shepherd, I shall not want.*
>
> Psalm 23:1 (KJV)

I knew right then, that everything was orchestrated by Jesus. Everything fell together perfectly. Eleven days after my car stopped running; my son and I were driving a new and safe vehicle.

Unforeseen occurrences befall us all, but once you see Him continually coming to your rescue, you gain confidence that He is always there, no matter what you are experiencing.

Jesus compares His caring for us like a hen that gathers her chicks under her wings. Hens brood over their baby chicks. One definition of brood is: *(of a bird) to warm, protect, or cover (young) with the wings or body.*[1]

They also guide them, with their wings, to food and shelter. That's exactly what Jesus wants to do for us, if we let Him. There is nowhere else that I'd rather be than tucked under Jesus' wing.

---

[1] "brood." *Dictionary.com Unabridged.* Random House, Inc. http://dictionary.reference.com/browse/brood (accessed: March 21, 2013).

Chapter 7

Turning to Elisha

THE TIME WAS 6:00 A.M., the year 2007, the day Thursday, January 11. I was spiritually starving and needed a heaping dose of encouragement. In an attempt to satisfy my need, I began searching for an inspirational program on television. As I flipped through the channels, I stumbled upon an evangelist whom I had not seen previously. As I was primping for work, I stopped to listen for a moment and was captivated by his sermon. He was saying what I was basically feeling, spiritually, that great things were about to take place in 2007. He said, "This is the year that God is healing and turning things around." He also said, "This is the year for a shift, and the last shall be first." Then he said, "You will look for the bad in your life and it will be gone."

I was so intrigued that I watched him the next morning and then again the following Monday. His message was the same, but progressed in detail. That particular morning, he said, "2007 is the year for the great anointing to be used to help deliver God's people." He continued, "In 2006, you went through a lot of tribulation so that your anointing could be complete. In 2007, it is the year of completion, and doors will be opened. The devil tried to kill you in 2006, but God pushed you through to 2007."

Wow! He hit the nail on the head because the enemy did try to kill me in more ways than one—that's another story—while I was completing a book for publication. He then said, "In 2007, God is giving you the power to rebuke your own winds. It is the year of completion, not the year of complaining. It is the year of power. Like Joseph, when God is finished with you, he will present you … from the pit to the palace. A pit cannot hold the anointing, but only for a season." Whew! I'm getting chills all over again telling this to you. "The pit is only there for your training. It's a preparation."

Why did he mention Joseph? It touched me deeply because Joseph is one of my favorite prophets in the Bible. I can relate to him so well, and I've loved him since I was a child. I used to watch his story on television. When his brothers put him in the pit and then sold him to the Egyptians, I cried and cried. When he became Pharaoh's right hand and ruled over the land, I was elated. I love his goodness, his wisdom, and his love for—and obedience to—God.

He also kept mentioning Elisha and the power that Elisha had in his anointing, which impressed upon me heavily. I had a feeling that I should read about him, but I did not.

Saturday, January 20, less than a week after hearing his sermon regarding Elisha, my six year old son, Colby, and I got into our old beat-up, ready-to-fall-apart car and headed out to look for a new one. Well, shortly after we got into the car—I'd only driven a couple of miles—my son began to sing a melody that he made up in his head, "mm...mm...mm...m...we're turning to Elisha." I swiftly turned around in amazement, "What did you say, Colby? Where did you hear that name?"

"I don't know mommy," he replied.

"Did you hear that name on T.V.?" I badgered.

"No," he answered.

"Do you have a friend at school named Elisha?"

"No," he answered again.

His face looked puzzled. He didn't understand why I was making such a big fuss over his little song.

This evangelist had just spoken of Elisha, and Colby had no clue as to who Elisha was. He had never heard his name on television and never heard me mention him. When I watched him on television, it was early in the morning while Colby was still in bed asleep. At that time, we lived in a single-wide trailer. His room was on one end and mine on the other. There is no way he heard the program. I knew then that Jesus was telling me to read about Elisha. I knew I would need to know something about him for a reason.

I continued driving to my daughter's apartment in my raggedy car, which I was content with, but I needed to replace it, lest I begin entertaining the possibility of walking to work. It was a small two-door car made in 1994. There was a big piece broken off of the dashboard. I had to shove a piece of Popsicle stick under the engine hood, so it would close properly. The rear view mirror was missing. There were many problems with this car; however, I made the best of it and thanked God for my ride.

We rode to the dealership with my daughter just in case I drove off with a new car. I wasn't very hopeful. I knew my credit was in bad shape, but I still went through the motions. We looked at all the cars. I set my eyes on one in particular, but kept perusing the lot, as it seemed out of my reach. I saw others that I liked, but the price was too high, or they were missing one thing or another. I went back to the car I loved at first.

"Okay, I'll try for this one," I informed my daughter.

She said, "Okay, let's go."

We walked into the building to speak with a representative. We sat down and told him which car I was interested in purchasing. They did some finagling, as I sat on pins and needles.

"Okay, Alice, can you put down one thousand dollars?"

I was quoted three thousand over the phone.

"Yes!"

"Okay, your payments will be three hundred fifty-four a month."

I was quoted over four hundred a month over the phone.

They called my insurance company, transferred coverage to my new car, handed me the keys, and said, "Here you go. You're all set."

What?! That was too easy. I just wanted to hurry and leave before they changed their minds. I excitedly drove out of the parking lot, following my daughter home.

As I drove, I thanked God for what he had done. I looked around my car in amazement. This car that Jesus blessed me with was fully loaded. It had a leather interior, cruise control, sunroof, and a rear view mirror complete with a digital compass. When I drove my new car to work, a co-worker said, "You have a spoiler on the back of your car." The light went off in my head and, immediately, Holy Spirit gave me the feeling of *Spoil Her*. I thought, "Jesus is going to spoil me." He continued to do just that, spoil me.

Just as this evangelist said, I was seeing things change in my life in a major way in 2007. In January, I had won a writing contest in an inspirational book, and my short story, *Jesus' Saving Arms*, was published in *Praise Reports: Inspiring Real-Life Stories of How God Works Miracles Today* published by Xulon Press.

Concerning Elisha, after that day, I sat and read about his unwavering faith. What I learned took my faith to another level.

God told Elijah to go and anoint Elisha to succeed him as Prophet. Upon doing so, Elisha dropped everything and followed Elijah, immediately (see 1 Kings 19:15–21).

Elijah performed all sorts of miracles. He was so dear to God that God did not allow him to die; instead, He took him up in a whirlwind.

Elijah told Elisha to stay where they were at; the Lord has sent him to Jordan. Elisha insisted on following him there. When they arrived at the Jordan, Elijah took his cloak, rolled it up and struck the water with it. The water divided to the right and to the left, and the two of them crossed over on dry ground.

> *When they had crossed, Elijah said to Elisha, "Tell me, what can I do for you before I am taken from you?"*
>
> *"Let me inherit a double portion of your spirit," Elisha replied.*
>
> *"You have asked a difficult thing," Elijah said, "yet if you see me when I am taken from you, it will be yours—otherwise, it will not."*
>
> *Suddenly, as they were walking along and talking, a chariot of fire and horses appeared and separated the two of them, then Elijah went up to heaven in a whirlwind. Elisha saw this and cried out, "My father! My father! The chariots and horsemen of Israel!" Elisha saw him no more; then, he took hold of his garment and tore it in two.*
>
> 2 Kings 2:9–12

Asking to inherit a double portion of Elijah's spirit was a tall order! I don't believe that Elijah said it was a difficult thing because it was hard for God to give it to Elisha. I believe he said so because a great deal of responsibility came with being anointed with that much spirit.

Did Elisha inherit a double portion of Elijah's spirit? We can see that he did in the next verses:

> Elisha then picked up Elijah's cloak that had fallen from him and went back and stood on the bank of the Jordan. He took the cloak that had fallen from Elijah and struck the water with it. "Where now is the LORD, the God of Elijah?" he asked. When he struck the water, it divided to the right and to the left, and he crossed over. The company of the prophets from Jericho, who were watching, said, "The spirit of Elijah is resting on Elisha." And they went to meet him and bowed to the ground before him.
>
> 2 Kings 2:13–15

After receiving this anointing, Elisha was unstoppable. He performed all sorts of miracles. On one occasion, a woman's young son took ill and shortly after, he died on his mother's lap. She was distraught, so she went to get Elisha.

> When Elisha arrived, the boy was lying on the couch. Elisha lay upon the boy, mouth to mouth, eyes to eyes, hands to hands. As he stretched himself out upon him, the boy grew warm. Elisha got up, walked back and forth in the room, and then stretched out upon him again. The boy sneezed seven times and opened his eyes.
>
> 2 Kings 4:32–35

See if you can wrap your mind around this:

> Elisha died and was buried. Now Moabite raiders used to enter the country every spring. Once while some Israelites were burying a man, suddenly they saw a band of raiders; so they

> *threw the man's body into Elisha's tomb. When the body touched Elisha's bones, the man came to life and stood up on his feet.*
>
> 2 Kings 13:20–21

Elisha's anointing was so powerful that even after he died, a man was raised from the dead by coming in contact with his bones. We receive according to the measure of our faith; our faith, however, moves us to act. His faith moved him to ask for a double portion of Elijah's spirit. He received it, and we can see the outcome.

A couple of years after I was introduced to Elisha, I was sitting at my desk at work when I received a phone call from my oldest son, "Ma, Randy got hit by a car."

"What? Is he okay?" My heart started racing.

"I don't know. He was riding his moped to work and a van hit him. He was thrown from his bike onto the pavement."

"Did you see him?"

Although, I was afraid of his possible response, I was compelled to ask.

"Yea, someone at my job told me that they saw him after he got hit, so I left work and ran out to go see for myself. When I arrived, he was just lying there, and there were cop cars and an ambulance around him."

Oh my God! That is the last thing you ever want to here on the other end of the telephone line. I was terrified.

"It's pretty bad. They sent for a helicopter. They're airlifting him to Greenville Hospital," he continued.

They flew him an hour away to a bigger, more advanced, facility due to the severity of his injuries, as well as him incurring trauma to his head.

I left my job immediately and drove to the hospital to go and be with him. My oldest son and my daughter met me there.

Randy is my middle son, who was in his late twenties at the time. He is my lighthearted child. He's always joking around and making me laugh. He has such a mild spirit. I really love that about him.

During my entire drive there, I prayed. This is one of those occasions when being a single mom proves to be extremely difficult. I had no co-parent to turn to during this tragedy. There was no one to hold my hand or understand how it felt to receive such devastating news regarding my child. Sure, I had my children, and my coworkers expressed concern, but there's no pain like a mother's pain. It would have been nice to have a caring father around to soften the blow, someone who has shared a parental bond with your child, but there was no father to be found. Well, let me rephrase that, no earthly father; Heavenly Father was there watching and comforting the entire time.

When I arrived, my oldest son and daughter were there. We walked up to the intensive care unit together with grave anticipation. A nurse directed us to his bed. My daughter and I stood on one side of the bed; my oldest son stood on the other. He was lying unconscious from being heavily sedated. He was hooked up to monitors and his face was covered with stitches sporadically placed; a few small ones on the side of his face, some on his forehead, and one large one on his chin. All of his wounds were camouflaged with dry patches of blood. He looked helpless, and I felt hopeless.

I spoke to him to let him know we were there, but I didn't think he could hear me. The nurse said, "Keep talking to him, so he can wake up."

So, I did. I kept talking, and finally, he slowly lifted his eyelids like they were heavy weights. Upon getting a glimpse of his iris, I said, "Hi", with a great big smile as to look optimistic. I didn't want the fright that was deep within to show on my face.

He looked at us, but he wasn't very coherent. He drifted back off as soon as we gave our hellos.

Soon they wheeled him to a private room, where he stayed for the next few days. After visiting for a while, I went home, and when I returned the next morning, the chalkboard in his room read:

Nurse: Elijah

All my fears dissipated. Naturally, Elisha came to mind. The anointing that was upon them and the power that they exerted was comforting to me at that moment. I knew, then, without a shadow of a doubt that my son was going to pull through and be fine. I took on the faith of Elisha, immediately.

When I actually met Elijah, the nurse, he was a sweet young man with a kind spirit. I told him that I was strengthened by Elijah and Elisha in the Bible. He informed me that he had a brother, who was named Elisha.

"No way," I said.

"Yes, my mom named us after those two prophets."

A few days later, my son came to my house, so I could care for him. He was healing nicely, but it took a few days for him to speak sensibly, and he slept a lot because he had swelling in his brain.

Once it went down, he was much better. Today he is healthy and attending college.

This child was on a moped, with no helmet or protective gear whatsoever, and was hit head-on by a van. He was thrown onto the pavement where he banged his head. He did not incur any brain damage, not one broken bone, only bruises and cuts. Tell me you don't believe that angels are here protecting God's children … I do!

Having the faith of Elisha can accomplish so many things in your life, as we shall further see.

Chapter 8

An Amazing Gift

It had been a year since I moved into the single-wide trailer with Colby. I let my oldest son take over the apartment after he came home from the military. It was getting crowded and I needed to find an inexpensive place for my four-year-old son and myself.

It all started when I quit my stable job of seven years to open a hair salon. I prayed long and hard about it before I actually quit. When I was getting down to the wire of making my final decision, I asked, "Am I really supposed to be doing this, Lord?" That night, after praying, God told me, in my spirit, to read Psalm 91. I don't think I had ever read it before, and I certainly didn't know what was in there. I opened my Bible and began reading. It was all about putting trust in the Lord and how He is our refuge.

> *He shall cover you with His feathers,*
>   *and **under His wings you shall take refuge;***
> *His truth shall be your shield and buckler.*
>
> *For He shall give His angels charge over you,*
>   *To keep you in all your ways;*
> *In their hands they shall bear you up,*
>   *Lest you dash **your foot against a stone**.*
>
> Psalm 91:4,11–12 (NKJV)
> **emphasis mine**

I will not strike my foot against a stone. "Are you telling me, Jesus, you will not let my foot strike against a stone? You will not let me fall?" As far as I was concerned, I had my answer. I slept calmly and peacefully that night. The next day, I went to work and put in my two weeks' notice.

I opened my salon. One year and four months went by, and business was not great. I had lots of clients, but not enough to pay for two sets of bills: apartment rent/salon rent, apartment electricity/salon electricity, apartment phone/salon phone. Well, you get the point. It became impossible bringing in ten thousand dollars, annually. Then, there was the concern of health insurance. I began to pray, "Jesus, I really need a job, so that I can get benefits and pay my bills. What if Colby gets sick?"

Not long after pleading my case, I ran into an ex coworker from the company I left to open my salon.

"Alice, so-and-so is leaving the company. They need another CSR to replace her. You should go and apply."

The following Monday, I went to the human resources department to apply for the customer service representative position. Within one week, I was back at my old job. When my supervisor assigned me a phone extension, he said, "Does this number sound familiar?"

"Uh, yes, isn't it my old extension?"

"Yea, it's the same extension you had before."

When I began to set up my voicemail, it was *already* set up. It had been a year and four months, and my voice-mail message that I set up years ago was still there waiting for me. I knew that my job was reserved, by Jesus, for me.

For the next year, I continued to work part-time at the salon. I would get off of work, pick up Colby at daycare, and then we'd go to the salon together. Those were very long days for the both of us, but he was such a good boy. He never complained.

However, it was still monetarily difficult, and I needed to find a place for Colby and me to live. We found a single-wide trailer to rent. It was small, but affordable.

Running a business, while working full-time, proved to be extremely challenging and very exhausting. In addition, I was so far behind in my salon rent that it would be nearly impossible to catch up. I finally had to let it go, so I closed the salon.

Now, you may be thinking, "Why did Jesus tell you to quit your job and open a salon only to have you go *back* to your job and close the salon two and one half years later? Sounds like you failed to *me*."

Did I fail? No. Like Psalm 91 said, God had me the entire time. He did not let my foot hit against a stone. When I closed the salon, I was excused of all back rent, leaving me with zero debt to the landlord.

I trusted in Jesus, obeyed him, and he protected me from harm.

"Yea, but what was the point? What did you gain?" you may be asking.

Well, we can't always figure out the *whys* of Jesus' direction; however, while I was at my salon, a young lady sat in my chair. As I styled her hair, we chatted about writing. I informed her that I had been working on a book off and on for the past umpteen years. I told her that I really wanted to get it published. She referred me to a local author who had recently published a book of her own. I contacted this accomplished author. She was very accommodating. She gave me her publisher and told me all I needed to know to get the job done.

Now this was major because this is a book that Jesus instructed me to write many years prior. I did not know if I would ever be able to finish it, let alone publish it, and now Jesus was handing me a publisher on a silver platter, which meant *it's time*.

If only to find a publisher for a book that may help *one* person seek God, that was a good enough reason to quit my job, open a salon, and go back to my job only to close my salon. God works in wondrous ways. I gained a lot of joy and experience at the salon, as well. I wouldn't change a thing.

Since I did not have the salon any longer, I had more time and more energy to concentrate on my book. It was my main focus. I would get up around 5:30 A.M. every morning to bang on the keys before I went to work.

My environment was humbling. The trailer I stayed in was very old. It had some major problems, but I wasn't concerned with having something better. Instead, I *made* it better. It was the prettiest inferior little trailer you'd ever want to see. I decorated it with pride and made it our home with all my favorite décor. I purchased pretty plates, sassy silverware, dining room chair covers, shimmering curtains, and surrounded my bed, which was two mattresses on the floor, with white sheers hanging from the ceiling. I was content, and I thanked God for what I had.

In a cozy little corner in my room, where my computer sat on a hand-me-down desk, all I cared about was finishing the book that Jesus told me to finish.

Close to my book being completed, I decided I needed an author photo. I went to get my makeup professionally done the day of the photo shoot.

Colby and I drove up the winding road; there was a grand, black, cast-iron gate that we had to pass through to get to the makeup artist's house. Through the gate were miles of green golf course, small ponds strategically scattered, and beautiful houses lined up along the road. We drove up her driveway and entered her home. She had two little girls. She had a large two-story house, which was yellow on the exterior. The interior walls were painted bright yellow, as well. It was stunning.

While I was getting my makeup done, Colby was having a great time playing upstairs with the girls in their playroom. When it was time to leave, Colby said, in front of the owner, "Mom, when we get a house, I want it to be yellow with an upstairs."

I looked at him, somewhat embarrassed because I didn't think that was going to happen—I hadn't even given it a single thought—and I didn't quite know how to respond.

"Okay, Colby, we'll see," followed by a nervous chuckle.

After that, when my manuscript had been submitted to the publisher, and I was proofing the galley, I felt that Jesus was telling me it was time to move. "Okay Lord, I know you want me to move now, but where? Am I supposed to get an apartment? Rent a house?" Never did it occur to me that I should look into purchasing a home because my credit was shot to ... well, you know.

By the way, it's the year 2007, the year that I was going to move from the pit to the palace; the year that everything in my life would turn around; and the year that I was introduced to Elisha's faith.

I remembered a name that another one of my clients gave me while at the salon. She purchased a house and went through a wonderful woman at the bank.

You know what? As I am telling you this, it just occurred to me that I found the woman I went to see about purchasing a home while at my salon. Opening it helped me gain more than just a publisher. Let me continue ...

I made an appointment and went to see her. I sat in front of her desk with pessimism. I answered all her questions as she jotted my answers down on a form. With each question, I thought, "That's going to kill it for me." I had the attitude of, "I don't even know why I'm here. They're going to turn me down." Up until then, I was always turned down for loans; always a "No," never a "Yes." Naturally, that's what I expected.

When we were done, she enthusiastically said, "I have a gift. God gave me the gift of getting people into homes. I love it. I work really hard for them and they end up buying homes. You're going to get a loan. You deserve it."

"Huh?"

Then she stood up and hugged me before I left.

She did not know me from Eve. She did not know of my relationship with God and that was her basis for me getting this loan ... God.

For the next two weeks, I patiently, anxiously waited for her response. Well, my patience ran out; I called her.

"I'm sorry," she said. "I've been so busy. I should have an answer for you very soon."

"Okay, that's fine," I said.

Within the next day or two, I saw an email from her in my inbox. The subject was "Good News". When I opened it, the content said, "You've been approved."

My word! I couldn't believe it. It was the most amazing email I'd ever received.

I found a real estate agent and began looking for a house right away. Within a month or so, I found a house, but when the agent and I went to look at it, I got a really bad vibe. There was graffiti painted on the stop sign at the top of the street, which really sent a bad message. After that, I stopped looking for a couple of weeks—my spirits were low—then I got motivated again. I was searching the houses listed online and saw a mint green house that was super cute! I called my real estate agent immediately and asked if we could view it.

As she was driving me to the location, I looked around and my eyes fell upon a sign in the road: *Alice Street.* I was taken aback. I know that God said not to look for omens, but he speaks to each of us in a different way. He knows me and shows me things in ways I can understand, and He will do the same for you.

When I saw that, it touched my spirit, and I said to Him, "Are you telling me that this is where I am going to live?"

On the next street down, we pulled into a cul-de-sac. We went into the little mint green house. It was adorable! I loved it and decided that was the house for me. Once we stepped back outside, we realized that each and every house in the cul-de-sac was newly built and only three out of eight were occupied. It was like finding a gold mine.

"Wow, all of these houses are brand new and empty!" I said.

My real estate agent was just as stunned and excited as I was. She didn't realize this location existed.

"Can we look in all the houses?" I asked.

"Sure, I have a master key that will open every one of them."

I was like a kid in a candy store. They all looked so delicious, but

I still had to be realistic and stick to a bite-sized one. I mean, that's all I could get right? I'm a single parent with a fairly low income. Single parents don't live in large houses, right?

Now see, this is the mentality that is drilled into our subconscious. This is the syndrome that I am trying to shatter.

We drove back to her office, all lit up and bursting with energy. When we arrived, she pounced on her computer and her fingers started dancing on the keys.

"Okay, let's check these out, get prices, and put in a bid."

When she looked at the mint green house, it showed up as being under contract.

"Alice, the green house you wanted is under contract already. Do you want to try for the brown one?"

"Yea, let's look at that one."

It was a mid-sized house. They were all very beautiful.

"This one is a little more than your loan. Let's look at the yellow one."

Well, I really thought that would be the impossible one because it was a larger home.

"Okay, let's look at it."

"Alice," she said in excitement, "this one is in your price range, *and* it's not even listed yet! These are contracted on a first-come, first-served basis, so you have a greater chance of getting this house."

"Okay, great," she had me all excited!

She got busy with her little paperwork stuff, "Sign this and this; and we gotta submit this and that …"

A few days later, she phoned me to tell me I got the house.

Everything seemed to be going well; however, we weren't on the homestretch, yet. The mortgage loan officer needed much documentation from me. She was all about business, and you just had to follow her instructions, "Get me your last four pay stubs, the last three years of your tax return. Get me this and that…"

I diligently got every stitch of information required. I couldn't even believe I had it readily at my disposal. I'm not usually that organized. Finally, she had everything she needed, and I played the waiting game.

Nope, one more thing; I now needed something from her.

"The seller is asking for the interest rate and pay schedule. Without it, I cannot get the contract."

"We need the contract to give you the pay rate and schedule," she responded. "Get it from them."

Neither side was budging. I became very discouraged, to say the least, and could have easily given up on purchasing the house.

I went home that evening to my little trailer. I sat on my bed, very downhearted and low in spirit. Nonetheless, something deep inside of me wouldn't let me give up. I sat and I prayed, and I started mustering up faith, "That is MY house. I AM going to have that house. Jesus gave it to me. He built it for me." Then the faith of Elisha came to mind, "If Elisha said, "Give me the interest rate and pay schedule, it would have been done."

> *And the water has remained pure to this day, according to the word Elisha had spoken.*
>
> 2 Kings 2:22

The next day, I had a new attitude. I decided I wasn't going to ask for it. I sent a bold, but kind, e-mail stating that I would hate to lose that property because the seller did not have the paperwork needed. I told her it was perfect for my son and me, and that I had not found anything else remotely close to it.

She said, "Okay."

Within minutes, she faxed the rates to me, and in turn, I faxed them to the seller. The next day, I called the seller to check on it, and was told that the contract was approved!

I don't think it was so much what I said to her, rather it was the faith and confidence I had behind what I said. It was the conviction.

When Colby and I moved in, it all dawned on me; this is the yellow house with an upstairs that the faith of a child requested and the house number, 2001, is Colby's birth year. No one can tell me that's not God!

I learned so many lessons from that single experience.

First, I appreciated the *humble* home, the little trailer, that God provided. I was thankful, and then He blessed me with more. We read in 1 Thessalonians 5:16–18 that we are to *"Rejoice always, pray continually, give thanks in **all** circumstances; for this is God's will for you in Christ Jesus."* (**emphasis mine**)

Second, I was focused on doing God's will when I was approved for a loan—writing *Saved by Grace, A Gift from God*. Jesus taught us in Matthew 6:33 (NKJV) to *"seek first the Kingdom of God and His righteousness, and all these things shall be added to you."*

Third, Colby is the one who spoke our house into existence. We must have faith of a child. Jesus said in Matthew 19:14, *"Let the little children come to me, and do not hinder them, for the kingdom of heaven belongs to such as these."*

Fourth, I gained further confirmation that having the spirit and attitude of Elisha can be powerful.

Fifth, I learned the importance of obedience to God. Jeremiah 7:23 tells us, *"Walk in obedience to all I commanded you, that it may go well with you."*

The day I was moving into my house, May 2, I received a call from a woman at my job, "Alice, guess what just came in the mail for you?"

I asked, "What?"

"Your book. I have the box right here on my desk!"

I was, actually, sitting on the floor in my new house opening a box, and she was opening my box of books on her desk.

I knew that Jesus was saying, "The reason you are moving in this new house is because you were obedient and published the book, good and faithful servant."

Single moms all over the globe are building and purchasing homes, regardless of the economy. A friend of mine, also a single mom, purchased a house before me. I saw it and began to have faith it was possible. Then *I* purchased *my* brand new house. Another single mom, and friend, came to see my house and began to have faith that is was possible; then *built* a house. It just keeps getting better and better!

We all connected and gained faith, one from the other. Now I'm connecting with you and hope that you will gain the same faith. Believe me, it *is* possible. If other single moms can do it, so can you.

The reason? Matthew 19:26 says: *"Jesus looked at them and said, 'With man this is impossible, but with God all things are possible.'"*

Part IV

LIVING BEYOND VISION

Chapter 9

THE POWERFUL SEVEN

ALTHOUGH I DID not realize it, while caring for my children and living from day to day, problem to problem, and solution to solution, I was applying principles in my life that led me to single-mom success.

I was afraid to have Colby because I thought raising him alone would be too difficult. But Isaiah 41:13 proclaims, *"For I am the LORD your God who takes hold of your right hand and says to you, Do not fear; I will help you."* I cast out fear and set in motion certain guidelines, which made it easier than I could ever imagine. Not to mention, I was blessed with a wonderful son. He's an "A" Honor Roll Student, which won him the Golden Presidential Award.

These certificates were awarded to children that have held an A average from the second to fifth grade; that's just one award among the fifty he has earned since kindergarten. See, you never know what a 'fetus' will accomplish if you give them half a chance.

As I look back, there are seven principles that carried me through, and they continue to guide my course today:

1) ACCEPT AND TAKE RESPONSIBILITY

I had to accept the fact that I was pregnant. In allowing myself to embrace the new baby, what came with it was responsibility. I was responsible in caring for this new life.

You can place the absent parent on child support; however, you can't squeeze blood from a stone. You may not get funds from them immediately, or at all for that matter; so, you must make up your mind that you are going to work and do all you can to support your child. When I divorced my three older children's father, I remember going into the courtroom feeling like a criminal. I felt as though the judge's sympathy was toward my ex-husband. She ordered him to pay fifty dollars a week for three kids. I couldn't believe it. I received, approximately, three checks total after that, and then they stopped completely. I went back to the court system to file a complaint, but nothing ever transpired. I never received another check during the entire time they were growing up.

I worked two jobs for many years. You have to do what you have to do to make certain your children are fed. Of course, I'm referring to positive avenues. There are many upstanding jobs that you can obtain, and everyone has special gifts and talents.

If you absolutely feel as though you cannot care for your child, there are many loving families seeking to adopt.

2) Forgive

If you are a single mom because someone ran out on you, you must forgive them. You must forgive so you can move forward.

Fourteen years after my husband and I divorced—the circumstances leading up to our divorce were abusive and horrendous—he contacted me. Keep in mind, he never helped us financially, and we didn't see him for years after the divorce. He abandoned us, and then showed up eight years later at my oldest son's Navy boot camp graduation ceremony, shouting, "That's my son! That's my son!" from the bleachers. Was I mad? No.

Six years after the ceremony, my phone rang.

"Hello."

"Hello."

His voice was all too familiar; I remembered it as if I had just spoken with him yesterday.

"I just want to say "Hi." I wrote you a letter, but I wanted to call and tell you that I know I didn't do right by you. I wanted you to know that you were a great wife and mother, and I hope everything is okay."

"I'm great. Everything is fine. I forgave you a long time ago and hope only the best for you."

I was standing in my warm and cozy brand new home. I had peace. If I were harboring hatred or ill feelings, I would not have been able to grow and prosper as I did.

I'm not suggesting that you forgive and return to the individual so they can continue to hurt you. Clearly, if the person is a predator they are not good for you! Forgive, but *don't* forget what they put you through, so you don't allow it to happen again and again.

You truly do need to forgive people, in general. It makes for a happier and healthier life.

> *Bear with each other and forgive one another if any of you has a grievance against someone. Forgive as the Lord forgave you.*
>
> Colossians 3:13

3) BELIEVE

Believe that you are more than capable of being a good parent. Believe that you are someone special and you have a purpose no matter what anyone else tells you. Believe in Jesus and believe that He will help you care for your family. Believe that the impossible is possible. In other words, have faith.

> *Truly I tell you, if you have faith as small as a mustard seed, you can say to this mountain, "Move from here to there," and it will move. Nothing will be impossible for you.*
>
> Matthew 17:20

However, faith without works is dead (see James 2:17). So, along with having faith that God is going to see us through any issue that may arise, we must work in harmony with Him and do our part. We put our 10% in (I say 10% because even when we use all our might,

God's works are far greater than ours) and He puts in the rest.

Among your works, seek the Kingdom of God.

> *But seek first the Kingdom of God and His righteousness, and all these things shall be added to you.*
>
> Matthew 6:33 (NKJV)

I don't strive for riches or material possessions; I strive to do God's will. In doing so, I have gained many material blessings. The Bible says that a man, who strives for riches, stabs himself with many pains. Focus on Jesus, and He will bless you with your needs and beyond. In addition, His load is light.

If you have not accepted Jesus Christ into your life as your Lord and Savior, now would be an optimal time to do so.

4) CHANGE

When we do the same thing over and over again, and get bad results, it's time to welcome a different method. When you change the way you live, your life will change. When you respect yourself, others will respect you. When you begin to have confidence in yourself, others will have confidence in you. When you change the way you think—positively—positive people begin to come into your life.

> *And be renewed in the spirit of your mind; and that ye put on the new man, which after God is created in righteousness and true holiness.*
>
> Ephesians 4:23–24 (KJV)

5) Be Prayerful

Don't underestimate the power of prayer. Prayer delivers, heals, sustains, comforts and restores. Prayer brings about change.

> *Rejoice always, pray continually…*
>
> 1 Thessalonians 5:16–17

6) Be Thankful

Be thankful no matter what your situation. When you are thankful and content with what you have, you are blessed with more.

> *Give thanks in all circumstances; for this is God's will for you in Christ Jesus.*
>
> 1 Thessalonians 5:18

7) Persevere

Never, ever, ever give up! You may think that what you are going through is never going to end. It may take longer than you would like, but you'll come through a stronger person. Be joyful; trials work out, in you, endurance and maturity.

> *As you know, we count as blessed those who have persevered. You have heard of Job's perseverance and have seen what the Lord finally brought about. The Lord is full of compassion and mercy.*
>
> James 5:11

Consider it pure joy, my brothers and sisters, whenever you face trials of many kinds, because you know that the testing of your faith produces perseverance. Let perseverance finish its work so that you may be mature and complete, not lacking anything.

James 1:2–4

Chapter 10

APPLYING THE PRINCIPLES

1. What is going on in your life that you should accept and take responsibility for?

2. Is there anyone you need to forgive? Who are they? For what are you forgiving them?

3. What should you believe God will do for you and your family?

4. What can you pray for, and how can prayer help your situation?

5. How can you change what you're doing to improve your situation?

6. List the things in your life that you can be thankful for right now:

7. If you persevere and don't give up, what will be the end result?

Other Books by Alice Monterio

Saved by Grace, A Gift from God

Pep Stephen, I Live with My Mom

Contact the Author:
alicemonterio@gmail.com

CPSIA information can be obtained at www.ICGtesting.com
Printed in the USA
LVOW10s1515260713

344849LV00001B/168/P